Two Kinds

of

Righteousness

**The Most Important Message
Ever Offered to the
Church**

●

By

E. W. KENYON

E. W. KENYON
Author

Fifteenth Printing

ISBN 1-57770-009-0

TABLE OF CONTENTS

THE REASON WHY

The urge that makes one man a drunkard, another a philosopher . . . the restlessness that fills the dance hall and the gambling resort, the roadhouse and the movies, and all the other places of pleasure is the heart's search for reality, that universal quest of the ages, the spirit's search for the Holy Grail.

No one finds it until they contact the Man, Christ Jesus, and crown Him as the Lord of their life. That moment the search ends, They have arrived.

They may not be conscious of what it is, but they know that the pleasures that they once sought have lost their taste and attraction.

They did not know that the hunger was spiritual, that it was a search after something that only God can give.

No person reaches the place of rest in the spirit until they have made that contact.

Man is a spirit being. He has a soul. He lives in his body.

The real man can never be permanently satisfied with the things of the senses.

It is a fact that the boy or girl that finds this thing in the teen-age never sows wild oats, has no great urge for the dangerous pleasures of the world. They have something that answers that cry.

This book is a study. It is a solution of the spirit problem. It is the first time that anyone has attempted to enter the realm and meet man on his own ground.

We invite you to read it carefully.

We wish we could get in contact with every person who does. We want to know the reactions in your spirit.

We believe we have found the fount of eternal joy.

INTRODUCTION

They had been fishing all the afternoon, now they are seated before the fire place at the camp. They were close friends. After a bit of silence, he said to his pastor:

"Life has not been what I had dreamed it would be. I have never reached the goal that I set my heart upon in my younger days. I have never opened my heart to anyone about it, but I am going to tell you today.

"I have always been religious. I have been a teacher of Bible Classes. I have been a superintendent of Sunday Schools. I have been an educator since I left college, but all these years there has been a secret background of unreality.

"God has never been real to me. I have read the Gospels, I have lectured about them. But all the time there was a consciousness that I had not arrived.

"That address you gave the other night revealed to me the thing that I have needed. In the early days we were never taught about Eternal Life. It was "getting converted" and "joining the church". We were taught a little about Justification, but it was always a theological point of view. It had no sense of reality in it.

"When I understood that one could receive Eternal Life — the very nature of God, then I knew that this thing you have been telling us about Righteousness was real.

"Like a flash, my theology and theories were stripped away and I saw myself for the first time as I really was in God's sight.

"I had never honored what He had done in Christ.

"I had never known what He had done for me.

"I was a New Creation. I had the very life and nature of God.

"I hardly dared to say it, "I am the Righteousness of God."

"I had never confessed it before.

"I had never dared even think that I would ever be anything like that until after death.

"Sin Consciousness had held me in bondage all these years. Whenever anyone preached against sin, I said, "That's me."

"I knew sin. I had fought sin. I had suffered from its effects. But I did not know that when I was made a New Creation that the past had stopped being. I did not know that if I committed sin, I had an Advocate with the Father, Jesus Christ the Righteous. I did not know that when I was recreated I became the Righteousness of God in Christ.

"I thank you for what you have told me."

4

MAN AS HE IS

Man has no approach to God.

The sense of condemnation has given to him an Inferiority Complex that makes him a coward. It robs him of faith in himself, in man, in God and in His Word. This Sin Consciousness holds him in bondage.

He has no right to approach God. He knows he is not good enough to pray and have his prayers answered.

If he does pray, it is the prayer of desperation.

This has led him into philosophy. He could no more keep away from the subject of God and religion than a hungry man can keep away from food.

The sense of guilt, inferiority, failure and weakness makes him reason, and that reasoning we call philosophy.

Because of this, Hagel eliminated God entirely from his philosophy. To him, God was a great mass mind without any brain center, without any personality.

In his philosophy, he also eliminated Satan.

If there be no Satan, then there can be no sin. If there is no sin, there is no sin consciousness. This would be fine if it were true, but it is just sense knowledge seeking a way of escape.

Then there would be no heaven because there is no life after death. Man floats out into a universal mind and is absorbed by it.

There is no Resurrection of the body, no Judgment. Man simply disintegrates and becomes a part of the great whole. This is but the dream of a man who could not find God with his senses.

You can see why Christian Science grew out of Hagel's philosophy.

If there is no Satan, there is no disease and no death. Yet they all die.

This is Sense Knowledge seeking for liberty and freedom that only God can give to man.

Man has a highly developed Sin Consciousness, a spirit inferiority complex, a sense of unworthiness that dominates him.

He is doubt ruled.

All he has is Sense Knowledge faith that cannot know God nor find Him.

This is man as he is.

Chapter I

WHY WE HAVE FAILED

HE church has been very strong in teaching man his need of Righteousness, his weakness and inability to please God.

She has been very strong in her denunciation of sins in the believer.

She has preached against unbelief, world conformity, and lack of faith, but she has been sadly lacking in bringing forward the truth of what we are in Christ, or how Righteousness and faith are available.

Most of our hymns put our redemption off till after death.

We are going to have rest when we get to heaven.

We are going to have victory when we get to heaven.

We are going to be overcomers when we get to heaven.

We are going to have peace with God when we get to heaven.

There will be no more failings when we get to heaven.

We have nothing on this side except failure, misery, disappointment and weakness.

What does He mean when He says, "Ye are complete in Him, who is the head of all principality and power"?

When are we to be complete? Is it in this life or in the next?

What does he mean in Rom. 8:37, "Nay, in all these things we *are* more than conquerors through him that loved us"?

When are we to be more than conquerors? Is it after death when we leave this vale of tears?

And Phil. 4.13, "I can do all things in him that strengtheneth me."

When is it that we are going to be able to do all things? Is it after we finish the course and stand with Him in the New Heaven and the New Earth?

He declares, Ro. 8:1 "There is therefore now no condemnation to them that are in Christ Jesus." When does this become ours?

We hear nothing but condemnation preached.

The ministry make no distinction between saint and sinner.

When does Rom. 5:1 become a reality?

"Being therefore declared righteous by faith, we have peace with God through our Lord Jesus Christ."

The ministers do not preach peace in the present. It is always in the future.

When are we to find this glorious thing called Peace? When is Jesus "made unto us wisdom from God, and righteousness and sanctification, and redemption"?

Is that to come to us at death, or is it a fact for us now?

"Him who knew no sin God made to be sin on our behalf; that we might become the righteousness of God in him."

We know the first part is true. But is the last part true?

Are we to become Righteous in the present life, or are we to become Righteous after death?

Is this Righteousness simply "reckoned" to us, or do we become Righteous in Him?

Is this Redemption metaphyscial or is it a reality?

Is Jude 24 to be depended upon?

"Now unto him that is able to guard you from stumbling, and to set you before the presence of his glory without blemish in exceeding joy."

Is that presence, of which He speaks here, before which we are to be set with exceeding joy—is that after death or is it now?

It seems very clear to me that we live in His presence now, that we walk in His presence now.

If He cannot present us "now" before His presence with exceeding joy, He certainly cannot present us before the presence of the Father after death with exceeding joy.

If it requires death to cleanse us from sin, we are left in an unhappy dilemma.

Death is of the Devil. It would indicate that God in His Redemption was unable to give us victory, that He needed the Devil to complete His redemptive work.

I believe that what the Scripture says about us is absolutely true, that God Himself is now our very Righteousness, and that we are the Righteousness of God in Him.

I am convinced that we are partakers of the Divine Nature.

There is no condemnation to us who "walk in the light as He is in the light."

The whole teaching of the modern church in regard to separation from the world is vague and illusive.

One branch of the church has taught that after we are Born Again we still have the "fallen nature" in us. That is the sin nature that came into Adam at the Fall.

What does this mean?

This Scripture will explain it. John 8:44, "Ye are of your father the devil."

It is Satan's nature. Satan has imparted to man his own nature.

They acknowledge the fact that God has provided a New Birth but that His New Birth is a flat failure.

The only thing He can do is to give us Eternal Life and forgive us. He cannot take the old nature out of us.

7

The whole thing is absurd. It is not true. It is not the Word.

2 Cor. 5:17, "Wherefore if any man is in Christ, he is a new creature: the old things are passed away; behold, they are become new. But all these things are of God, who reconciled us to himself through Christ."

A man cannot be in Christ and have the Devil's nature in him. He is either in the family of God or in the family of Satan.

I John 3:10, "In this the children of God are manifest, and the children of the devil."

There can be no real development of faith, no strong, victorious Christian life with this mixed conception.

We are either New Creations or we are not.

We have either passed out of death into life, or we have not.

When he says, "Sin shall not lord it over you"—he means exactly what he says.

If you live a life of weakness and defeat, it is because you do not know what you are in Christ.

The supreme need of the church at this hour is to know what we are in Christ, how the Father looks upon us, and what He considers us to be.

Read with great care Eph. 1:3, "Blessed be the God and Father of our Lord Jesus Christ, who has blessed us with every spiritual blessing in the heavenlies in Christ."

Col. 1:21-22, "Being in time past alienated and enemies in your mind in your evil works, yet now hath he reconciled in the body of his flesh through death, to present you holy and without blemish and unreprovable before him."

This has already been done in Christ. You stand before Him complete in Christ.

Eph. 5:27, "That he might present the church to himself a glorious church, not having spot or wrinkle or any such thing; but that it should be holy and without blemish."

In the mind of most people this is after death. But that is not true. We are presented without spot or without wrinkle now.

Do you think that any believer filled with sin (as that term is used) could be in Christ and stand before Him without spot or wrinkle?

If He cannot take the sin nature out of us when we are Born Again, if the merits of the blood do not reach this and wipe it out, then when can we ever be made right?

Not when we die, for Satan is the author of death.

I declare before the angels in heaven, before the demons and all the hosts of hell, that the Redemptive work of God needs no help from Satan to make us complete in God's presence.

8

Chapter II

REVELATION OF RIGHTEOUSNESS

W E understand that Righteousness means the ability to stand in the presence of the Father God without the sense of guilt or inferiority.

This has been the quest of the ages.

The desire to get rid of Sin Consciousness has given birth to all the major religions of the world.

Mrs. Eddy, copying Hagel, boldly declares that God is not a person, and that Satan is not a person. So, there being no God and no Devil, there could be no sin.

If there were no sin, there could be no judgment because of sin. If there were no sin and no fear of judgment, there would be no Sin Consciousness.

Our declaration that the tide does not rise, does not stop it from rising. The philosopher's declaration that God is not, does not stop God from being.

God is. Satan is. Sin is.

But God has dealt with the sin problem in His Son. He has put sin away by the sacrifice of that Son. He has made it possible on legal grounds for man who is spiritually dead, in union with Satan, to become a New Creation by receiving the very nature and life of God.

This life and nature of God is Righteousness. Consequently, the man who has received the nature of God has automatically become the Righteousness of God in Christ.

He may not know it, he may not take advantage of it, but it is true.

The dominion of Sin Consciousness over the Church has been fostered, developed, and made a reality by the ministers who have preached sin instead of preaching Christ and the New Creation.

Sin Consciousness came with the Fall when man became a partaker of Spiritual Death.

Down through the ages universal man has been under the blighting curse of Spiritual Death which gave birth to Sin Consciousness.

Spiritually dead man cannot stand in God's presence.

We see how God illustrated that fact in the Old Covenant.

The High Priest went into the Holy of Holies once every year, and then only when he was blood covered. The High Priest did not go into the Holy place to worship, but to make a yearly atonement for spiritually dead Israel.

God sent His Son to the world to become Incarnate, to become eternally united with humanity.

That Son went on the Cross by the determinate counsel of God, became sin, took our place as a Substitute. Then He conquered the Enemy and made Righteousness available to man.

A redemption that did not make man Righteous would be a fallacy.

Until man is Righteous and knows it, Satan reigns over him, sin and disease are his masters. But the instant he knows that he is the Righteousness of God in Christ and knows what that Righteousness means, Satan is defeated.

The Church has not taught even a limited Righteousness. It has a theological justification that does not meet the issue.

God's redemption in Christ is the solution. It makes man a dominant spirit where he has served as a slave in weakness.

How can we obtain this Righteousness that will give us perfect Fellowship with the Father, that will give us a consciousness of being masters over the forces of darkness?

That Righteousness comes to us by taking Jesus Christ as Saviour and confessing His Lordship over our lives.

When we know that Jesus died for our sins according to Scripture, that the third day He arose again from the dead after He had put our sin away and satisfied the claims of Justice as our substitute; when we know that and take Him as our Saviour and confess Him as our Lord, that moment we receive God's nature and we become the Righteousness of God in Christ.

2 Cor. 5:21 "Him who knew no sin God made to become sin on our behalf; that we might become the righteousness of God in him."

We have become the Righteousness of God in Christ.

This Righteousness is not an experience, although it gives birth to many marvelous experiences.

It is the nature of the Father imparted to us.

It is that nature gaining the ascendency in us until we know that we are what God says we are—masters, conquerors!

Chapter III

STUDY IN SIN CONSCIOUSNESS

O Sin Consciousness can be traced the reason for practically every spiritual failure. It destroys faith. It destroys the initiative in the heart. It gives to man an inferiority complex.

He is afraid of God. He is afraid of himself. He is ever searching to find someone that can pray the prayer of faith for him. He has no sense of his own legal right to stand in the Father's presence without condemnation.

The inferiority complex that is bred of Sin Consciousness is faced everywhere in the church.

It has been said to me many times, "If I could get rid of this Sin Consciousness, I'd get my healing. I'd be a power for God, but I can't get rid of it."

Has God provided a Redemption that cures this sin disease?

I am sure He has. If He hasn't planned to take it out of man during his earth walk, man can never stand right before God because Redemption works only in this age.

God has made provision to make a New Creation. He has planned to impart His own nature to him—taking out the old sin nature and replacing it with His own nature. This will destroy Sin Consciousness.

Few theologians have recognized the fact that Sin Consciousness is the parent of practically all human religions.

Man has sought to heal this awful disease.

The sense of unworthiness destroys faith, robs us of our peace of mind, makes ineffectual the most earnest and zealous prayer life.

It robs us of all fellowship and communion with the Father.

Our theologians since Luther have never found a cure for this condition. The Holiness people have attempted bravely to meet this issue, but so far they have never been able to permanently cure a patient.

Man's cure has been repentance of sins, sorrow for sins, and deep agony in prayer.

Others have tried to quiet their consciences by going to church, doing penance, fasting, giving money, saying prayers, doing good deeds, giving up pleasures, confessing their sins, fighting bad habits, putting themselves under discipline of self-denial and self-abasement, by neglecting the body. Some have even gone so far as to lacerate their bodies. Others have taken long pilgrimages.

All these methods have been tried. Every earnest spirit has attempted some of them.

A new movement has just arisen in which men and women are finding temporary relief in confessing their sins to one another.

Confessing sins may bring temporary relief from the pressure that is upon them, but no works of any kind whether they be works of self-abnegation, repentance, penance, saying of prayers, or self-denial can ever rid the heart of Sin Consciousness.

There are two kinds of Sin Consciousness. One is the man who has never been Born Again. The other is the undeveloped believer—one who has never grown beyond the state of babyhood, doesn't know his rights and privileges in Christ.

Where is the difficulty?

It is this. The natural man is a sinner, but he is more than that.

In 2 Cor. 6:14 he is called "iniquity." In other places he is called "sin".

He is more than a transgressor. He is more than a violater of the law.

He is by nature a child of wrath. He is spiritually dead. He is united with Satan as the believer is united with God.

The believer has become a partaker of God's nature, the natural man is a partaker of Satan's nature.

The problem is: How can God legally deal with the sin problem and the sins problem? How can He deal with this Satanic nature that is in man?

God's Cure

God has wrought a Redemption that covers every phase of man's need, perfectly restores his fellowship with the Father so that there is no sense of guilt or sin, no memory of past wrong-doing.

The believer stands complete in Christ. He has partaken of the fulness of God in Christ.

John 1:16 "For of his fulness have we all received, and grace upon grace."

If you read Hebrews 10:1-19 carefully, you will see that under the First Covenant there was a remembrance made of sins year by year, but in the New Covenant a man who has accepted Jesus Christ loses the sense of sin and in its place receives a sense of his oneness and fellowship with the Father.

Col. 1:13-14, "Who delivered us out of the authority of darkness and translated us into the kingdom of the Son of his love; in whom we have our redemption, the remission of our sins."

Notice in this Scripture that He "delivered us out of the authority of darkness"—that is Satan's dominion—and at the same time "translated us into the kingdom of the Son of his love."

There are four facts here.

First, we are delivered out of Satan's dominion.

Second, we are born into the kingdom of the Son of His love.

The third is, "In whom we have our redemption." That is a Redemption from Satan's dominion. Satan has no legal right to reign over the man who has accepted Christ as his Saviour. That man has been delivered out of Satan's dominion, Satan's family, Satan's authority. He· has been born into the family of God, the kingdom of the Son of His love.

When this was done the Redemptive work that Christ wrought became a reality.

Fourth, He not only redeems us out of Satan's dominion—there is also a remission of our sins.

He redeems us.

He recreates us.

He delivers us out of Satan's authority.

He remits all that we have ever done.

Chapter IV

WHAT RIGHTEOUSNESS MEANS

HERE is no other word in the Bible, or in theology, which is less understood and appreciated than this word. Yet enwrapped within it is everything for which humanity has craved.

This thing that Righteousness gives to man is the parent of all human religions. The gross, immoral religions of paganism, and the refined, cultured, philosophical religions of the modern day, are all the children of man's desire for the thing that Righteousness gives to him.

Righteousness restores to man all that he lost in the Fall, plus a new relationship as a son with all its privileges.

Let us notice just a few of the many things that Righteousness gives us as revealed in Christ's finished work.

Our Standing Is Restored

Righteousness comes to us in the New Creation. It restores our standing before God. It takes away the old Sin-Consciousness that has crippled and robbed us of all our spiritual initiative, confidence and assurance in His presence. It restores to man a standing before the Father on the same ground that Jesus enjoyed in His earth walk.

Remember the fearlessness of Jesus in the presence of the Father, His fearlessness before Satan.

He knew He had a legal right in the Father's presence. He knew He was Master of Satan and all his forces.

Remember how fearless He was in the storm, and what an absolute Ruler He was over the laws of nature.

He was not afraid to say to dead Lazarus, even in the presence of a large number of people, "Lazarus, come forth."

He had no sense of inferiority in the presence of death. He had no sense of inferiority in the presence of disease. He was not afraid to speak to the maimed and command them to become whole.

Righteousness is a masterful thing.

The problem is: Has God restored Righteousness to man? That is the reason we are writing this little book. We are trying to answer that age old problem.

Fellowship Is Restored

Righteousness restores to man his lost Fellowship.

We see that Fellowship illustrated in Jesus' life. He approached the Father with the same liberty and freedom as a child approaches his parent. He addressed the Father as familiarly and as simply as a child addresses his father.

Jesus enjoyed a unique Fellowship. There was no sense of guilt, no sense of sin, no sense of condemnation in Jesus' spirit.

Our hearts are asking today, "Can God restore such a Righteousness to man?"

We believe He can. We believe that the finished work of Christ guarantees it.

Jesus had no sense of lack. When He needed money to pay His poll tax, He told Peter to go and catch a fish and he would find the money in its mouth.

When He fed the multitude of five thousand, they handed Him five loaves and three small fishes. He blessed the bread and broke it. The multitude was fed and twelve basketsful remained.

He had no sense of lack of money. He had no sense of lack of love, lack of knowledge, or lack of ability in any line.

He had no sense of Sin-Consciousness. He had no Inferiority Complex.

This Righteousness that Jesus had, gave Him the sweetest, most perfect Fellowship with the Father.

Faith Is Restored

Righteousness restores to man his lost faith.

If you want to see this illustrated, go to the cities and see the congregations gather to hear men and women talk on psycho-analysis or, in other words, how to get faith in yourself so you can become a master over others who have no faith in themselves.

Jesus had no need of faith. He believed in Himself. He believed in His mission. He believed in His Father. And He must have believed in humanity.

If you want to see the necessity of restored Righteousness, go to our churches and see the utter faithlessness of the great body of Christendom.

They are like Thomas who said, "I will not believe until I can put my finger into the print of the nails in His hand, and thrust my hand into His side."

Thomas' faith, like that of the modern Christian, was Sense Knowledge faith. It is faith in what they can see and hear and feel.

This is the reason why some of the modern movements, which have so much physical demonstration, have challenged the faith of the multitudes.

It is Sense Knowledge faith.

Peace Is Restored

Only when Righteousness is restored can peace be restored. It restores our peace with God. The individual is like the mass. The mass is like the nation—seething, restless, having no peace and no quietness.

Isaiah 57:20-21 "But the wicked are like the troubled sea; for it cannot rest, and its waters cast up mire and dirt. There is no peace, saith my God, to the wicked."

The sense of lack, the sense of guilt, the sense of want, the consciousness of burdens and unpaid bills fill the heart with anxiety and restlessness.

Righteousness restores quietness and rest to the spirit. We are no longer afraid of bills, no longer afraid of circumstances.

Faith rises unconsciously and we face the most adverse conditions with a sense of superiority.

We are masters. There is nothing that man needs so much today as a sense of Righteousness.

Freedom Is Restored

It not only restores peace, but it gives man the thing for which the human heart has sought and struggled down through the ages—freedom.

The greatest freedom is not political freedom, freedom from financial worry or physical discomfort, but it is freedom from Sin Consciousness.

Righteousness restores freedom to man—the same kind of freedom that Jesus had—the kind of freedom that the human has craved above every other thing.

It is freedom in Christ, freedom from the fear of Satan, freedom from the fear of man because we trust in God with all our hearts. We lean not upon our own understanding. We are not harassed and depressed by Sense knowledge or by circumstances.

We stand in the sweet, wonderful consciousness of—"My Father is greater than all," and "Greater is He that is in me than he that is in the world".

Sonship Is Given

Righteousness gives us the sweet consciousness of sonship privileges.

We are sons. God is our Father. We are His children. We are in His family.

We know our Father. He loves us and we love Him.

Righteousness restores to us the joy, the unspeakable joy of Fellowship with heaven on terms of equality.

We are not servants. We are not sinners.

We are sons.

We are heirs of God and joint-heirs with Jesus Christ.

Chapter V

HOW GOD MADE US RIGHTEOUS

UR standing with God is on the ground of faith in Jesus Christ. In other words, God laid upon Jesus our iniquities.

2 Cor. 5:21, "Him who knew no sin God made to be sin on our behalf."

Jesus was more than a sin offering. He was actually made sin with our sins. He was made unrighteous with our unrighteousness.

As our Sin Substitute, bearing our sins and bearing us, He went to the place of suffering after He left His body. He stayed there until every claim of Justice against us had been satisfied.

He was our Substitute, taking our place, being made sin with our sin. He went to the prison to which sinners were sentenced and suffered until everything against us had been met.

It was Deity suffering for humanity, and being Deity He could pay the penalty.

When the Supreme Court of the Universe declared that what God had wrought in Christ was sufficient, that His sufferings were adequate and met every demand of Justice, He declared that Jesus was Justified or made Righteous. Ro. 4:25.

In 1 Tim. 3:16 Paul says that He was "justified in the spirit." and in 1 Pet. 3:18 we read that He was "made alive in the spirit."

He was born out of death, so that He is called again and again, "the first born from among the dead."

God laid our sin upon Him. He was made to be sin, made to suffer in our stead.

When He had met the demands of Justice, death could hold Him no longer.

He was "declared righteous."

He was "made alive".

He became the "firstborn from the dead"—the Head of a New Creation. Col. 1:18.

When we believe in Jesus Christ as our Saviour, God is able to declare us righteous on the ground of what Jesus did.

There are two phases to this Righteousness.

First, God declares us righteous; and second, we are made New Creations.

We become partakers of the Divine Nature, so that we are righteous by nature and righteous by faith.

Now we can understand 2 Cor. 5:21, "Him who knew no sin God made to be sin on our behalf."

Why? "That we might become the righteousness of God in him."

As surely as God made Jesus sin, God made us righteous the moment we accepted Him.

"Being justified freely by his grace (or, being made righteous freely by his grace) through the redemption that is in Christ Jesus."

He declares that we were made righteous freely by His grace through the redemption that was in Christ Jesus.

He did this "for the showing, I say, of his righteousness because of the passing over of the sins done aforetime, in the forbearance of God."

What does he mean by that?

From the time Adam fell until Jesus hung on the Cross, God had been covering sin with the blood of bulls and goats. Lev. 17:11 "For the life of the flesh is in the blood; and I have given it to you upon the altar to make atonement for your souls."

The word "atonement" means "to cover". It is never used in connection with the blood of Christ because the blood of Christ does not cover—it cleanses!

We do not need to be covered.

Under the Law, sin was not put away. It was not cleansed. It was only covered by the blood of bulls and goats.

Now by faith we can take Jesus Christ as our Saviour and Lord. When we do that we become the Righteousness of God in Him.

Being made righteous by His grace, we have peace right now with God through our Lord Jesus Christ.

Having been made righteous, having been declared righteous by the Supreme Court of the Universe, having had this fellowship restored that had been broken through the ages, the peace of God which passeth all understanding floods our beings. Ro. 5:1.

Now we can stand in His presence without any Sin-Consciousness, without any fear, because "as He is, so are we in this world."

He is righteous. He Himself has declared us righteous and made us righteous.

This is the foundation on which faith grows.

When we know this as the Word of God teaches it, we will step into the Father's presence without any challenge or question in our minds.

We know that there is therefore now no condemnation to us, because we are in Christ Jesus.

This was God's greatest problem.

How could God legally restore to man his lost Righteousness and still be just Himself?

The first eight chapters of Romans deal with this problem and give us the solution.

Eph. 2:12, "Having no hope and without God in the world." Fallen man is without God and without hope.

He is spiritually dead, a partaker of Satan's nature. He has no standing with God. He has no citizenship and no legal right of appeal. He is like a convict in a state penitentiary.

He is in union spiritually with God's enemy. His nature is enmity against God. He is not subject to the will of God, and cannot be until he is recreated. Ro. 8:7.

How could God reconcile man to Himself, make him righteous, and restore him to perfect fellowship?

It could only be wrought by God's own Son taking man's place, meeting every demand of Justice, and going down to the level of lost man. 2 Cor. 5:17-21.

This Jesus did and, after the claims of Justice had been perfectly met, He was justified in spirit.

Not only was He justified in spirit, but He was also made alive in spirit.

He was recreated so that God said of Him, "Thou art my Son, this day have I begotten thee."

When Jesus was declared righteous, justified, and made alive, then He was restored to perfect fellowship with the Father.

After He was restored to perfect fellowship with the Father and could enter heaven as though He had never been made sin, He sat down at the right hand of the Majesty on high.

He had made a perfect substitution for man.

He had made it possible not only for God to justify man, but also to perfectly recreate him.

On the ground of that, man was reconciled to God. Now he has a right to fellowship and commune with the Father— to stand in His presence as though he had never sinned.

The fact that Jesus could leave the abode of the lost and go directly into the Father's presence is proof that the vilest sinner can do the same through Jesus Christ our Lord.

It does not make any difference how wicked a man is, if he takes Christ as his Saviour and confesses Him as his Lord, God makes him a New Creation. That man becomes the Righteousness of God in Christ.

Righteousness becomes a living reality in him.

In the Garden, Adam had perfect fellowship with God. No work that God could do for man would be perfect unless it gave back to man his lost Righteousness, his lost privilege of fellowship and his lost dominion.

His lost Righteousness and his lost fellowship are restored in the New Creation.

The moment his Righteousness is restored, his lost dominion is also restored in the use of the Name of Jesus.

"If ye shall ask anything of the Father, he will give it you in my name".

The Righteous Man

"The Prayer of the Righteous Man" Jas. 5:16

You are the righteous man and your prayer avails much in its working.

Elijah had reckoned righteousness, a servant's righteousness. You have been made righteous by receiving the nature of the Father. There is no limit to your prayer life. You have within you now all the elements that are necessary to make you all that the Father dreamed that you would be in Christ.

Dare to pray; dare to use the name of Jesus; dare to take your place. Be as fearless as the Master was in His dealing with Satan and disease because you have His Name; you have His ability; He is now your wisdom and the strength of your life.

The secret of victory is acting fearlessly; confessing boldly for Satan fears you.

You are the righteous man.

Chapter VI

GOD HIMSELF OUR RIGHTEOUSNESS

THERE must be more in this subject of Righteousness than most of us have realized. We know it is the key of the Revelation given to Paul.

He said that he was not ashamed of the "Good News" for it not only gave to men salvation, but "therein is revealed a righteousness of God from faith unto faith." Rom. 1:7.

Then in Rom. 3:21-22, "But now apart from the law a righteousness of God hath come to light, being witnessed by the law and the prophets; even the righteousness of God on the ground of faith in Jesus Christ."

After stating the fact of our Redemption in Christ in this chapter, he makes a statement in the 26th verse, "For the showing, I say, of his righteousness at this present season: that he might himself be righteous and the righteousness of him that hath faith in Jesus." (Mar. Am. R.)

This is almost beyond our apprehension when God declares that He Himself has become our Righteousness.

Righteousness means the ability to stand in God's presence without the sense of guilt, condemnation, or inferiority.

A Redemption that would be worthy of God must accomplish this. Man has been estranged from God. He must be restored.

Lying behind this is the heart tragedy that man is the reason for Creation. When man sinned he separated himself from the fellowship of the Father.

The whole drama of Redemption is consummated in this— man must be restored to perfect fellowship with the Father and it must be done upon legal grounds.

Any Redemption that does not restore to man a perfect fellowship and a perfect relationship on legal grounds will not be worthy of the Father and will not lift man into the place that God has planned for him.

The object of Righteousness is to give man fellowship. Because of this the Incarnation took place, the public ministry of Jesus, and then the Cross where He was made sin.

He stayed under judgment until He was made Righteous. When He was made Righteous and given life, then He conquered our Adversary and arose from the dead.

We know He was made sin with our sin. We know He must have been made Righteous, because He entered into the Father's presence after His Resurrection as the head of the New Creation.

If He, who had been spiritually dead and made sin with our sin, could be made Righteous and restored to perfect fellowship with the Father, then on legal grounds God can recreate us and give us the same Righteousness and fellowship enjoyed by the Master.

Some Facts About Righteousness

Rom. 4:25 says, "Who was delivered up on the account of our trespasses, and was raised when we were declared righteous."

And Romans 5:1, "Being therefore declared righteous by faith, we have peace with God through our Lord Jesus Christ."

Peace is fellowship. Here is the declaration that when Christ arose from the dead, He arose because Righteousness had been set to our account.

When we accept Jesus Christ as Saviour that Righteousness becomes a part of our being because we become partakers of the Divine Nature. The Divine Nature is Righteousness, so we become Righteouswith His nature—His own Righteousness.

2 Cor. 5:17-19. "Wherefore if any man is in Christ, he is a new creation: the old things are passed away; behold, they are become new. But all these things are of God, who reconciled us to himself through Christ."

There is not only a perfect Righteousness, but also a perfect reconcilation.

Reconciliation means fellowship, for there can be no fellowship until there is reconciliation.

And the strange thing about it is, "And gave unto us the ministry of reconciliation; to wit, that God was in Christ reconciling the world unto Himself, not reckoning unto them their trespasses ,and having committed unto us the word of reconciliation."

Reconciliation comes to us through the New Creation. The moment we receive Eternal Life, our spirits are recreated. We become His very sons and daughters.

With the New Creation comes reconciliation and righteousness and fellowship.

The joy of the Christian life is fellowship with the Father. When we are in fellowship, faith flows to flood tide. When we are out of fellowship faith shrinks and is enfeebled.

Fellowship is maintained through the Word and the intercession of Jesus. He is our Advocate at the right hand of the Father.

Righteousness gives us our standing with the Father now, our right to the use of Jesus' Name now, our position as sons and daughters, and our victory over the Adversary.

The believer should be continually witnessing and confessing his righteousness and his fellowship in Christ.

Chapter VII

RIGHTEOUSNESS LEGALLY OURS

"**H**IM who knew no sin God made to become sin on our behalf; that we might become the righteousness of God in him."

God made Jesus sin. Sin was not only reckoned to Him, but His spirit actually became sin.

He died twice on the Cross.

Is. 53:9, marginal rendering, "And they made his grave with the wicked, and with a rich man in his deaths."

Note that "in his deaths" is plural.

He died spiritually the moment that God laid sin upon Him and made Him to become sin. He died physically hours later.

He died in spirit. Then it tells us in 1 Tim. 3:16 that He was justified in spirit, and in 1 Peter 3:18 that He was made alive in spirit.

As soon as He was justified, that moment justification belonged to the world for He was our substitute.

Romans 4:25, "Who was delivered up on the account of our trespasses, and was raised because (or when) we were justified."

When were we justified? When Jesus was justified.

When was Jesus justified? When He was made alive in spirit.

That explains two Scriptures. Acts 13:33-34 where God says, speaking of the Lord Jesus, "Thou art my Son, this day have I begotten thee", and Col. 1:15-18 "Who is the image of the invisible God, the firstborn of all creation . . . . And he is the head of the body, the church: who is the beginning, the firstborn from the dead."

Jesus was the first person ever Born Again.

He was the first born, and His birth out of death into life was for us.

Now we can understand Eph. 2:10, "For we are his workmanship, created in Christ Jesus."

When did He do that work? At the time of which I have just spoken—from the time He was made sin, justified, arose from the dead, carried His blood into the Heavenly Holy of Holies and sat down at the right hand of God.

He sat down because His work was finished, because the New Creation could become a reality.

Now men could pass out of death into life, could become the Righteousness of God in Him.

If Jesus was made righteous, and made so righteous that He could come out of hell and go into heaven; if He after being made sin could become so righteous that He could go into the Father's presence, sit down at His right hand, and be accepted there by the Father, then everyone who accepts Jesus Christ as Saviour, confesses His Lordship over him, and receives Eternal Life will become as righteous as Jesus is because Jesus was made unto us Righteousness from God.

Don't stop there. Dare to turn to Romans 3:26 and read the American Revision. ,

"That God might himself be righteous, and the righteousness of him that hath faith in Jesus."

There God declares that He Himself becomes the Righteousness of the man who has faith in Jesus as a Saviour and confesses Him as his Lord.

If we become the Righteousness of God in Christ—and Righteousness means the ability to stand in the Father's presence without condemnation and with absolute freedom—then God has solved the Sin Consciousness problem.

How God Deals With The Sin Problem

No man can stand right with God simply by having his sins pardoned. It would leave the old nature that produced those sins still master of the situation.

But when a man becomes a child of God, he is a New Creation.

"The old things are passed away; behold, they are become new. But all these things are of God, who reconciled us unto himself through Christ."

There is a perfect reconcilation. There could not be a perfect reconciliation if there was sin in this New Creation.

He has made man a new being.

At the same time everything man has ever done in his past life is remitted, wiped out as though he had never committed sin.

The word "remission" is never used in connection with the believer. It is always used in connection with the New Birth.

A man's sins are remitted only once.

Eight or nine times "aphesis" is translated "forgiveness". Forgiveness is never used in connection with the New Birth.

Take as an illustration 1 John 1:9, "If we confess our sins, he is faithful and righteous to forgive us our sins and to cleanse us from all unrighteousness."

This is not written to the unsaved man. It is written to the believer who has lost fellowship with the Father.

Forgiveness belongs to the believer.

Remission belongs to the sinner.

Notice carefully that the sin nature is eliminated and a new nature takes its place. All the sins that the Old Creation has ever committed are wiped out as though they had never been. God has no remembrance of them.

When a man tells you that you must confess the sins you committed before you were Born Again, he is ignorant of God's dealing with the sin problem. The New Creation has no sins and has no sin.

If he has sin, he has not been Born Again. If he has sins, his sins were never remitted.

Heb. 9:26 says, "Now once at the end of the ages hath he been manifested to put away sin by the sacrifice of himself."

Here we get God's statement in regard to sin. Man can become a New Creation because his sin nature was laid on Jesus.

When He was made sin and put sin away, the sin problem was a closed issue.

The most wicked man that ever lived can accept Jesus Christ, and the instant he does he becomes a New Creation. When he becomes a New Creation, the sin nature stops being and a new nature takes its place.

The New Creation

2 Cor. 5:17. We have used this Scripture once, but let us go into it once more carefully.

"Wherefore if any man is in Christ, there is a New Creation: the old things are passed away; behold, they are become new. But all these things are of God who has reconciled us unto himself through Christ."

Notice first, "Wherefore if any man is in Christ."

The expression "In Christ" means that when a man is Born Again he comes into Christ. As the branch is in the vine, so the believer is united with Christ.

Romans 6:5, "For if we have become united with him in the likeness of his death, we shall be also in the likeness of his resurrection."

There is our union with Christ. That union means that we are in Him.

So he says, "Wherefore if any man is in Christ, there is (or he is) a new creation."

It is not a problem of sins being forgiven, nor a problem of our having repented enough, but it is a problem of an actual New Birth.

Natural man is without God, without hope, spiritually dead, a child of the Adversary, and by nature a child of wrath. When he accepts Jesus Christ as his Saviour, confesses Him as his Lord, at once he is recreated by receiving Eternal Life, the nature of God.

John 10:10, "I came that they may have life, and may have it abundantly."

John 5:24 declares that he who believes on Him passes out of death into life and cometh not into judgment.

I John 5:12, "He that hath the Son hath the life."

Or I John 5:13, "These things have I written unto you, that ye may know that ye have eternal life, even unto you that believe on the name of the Son of God."

This is not a hope of Eternal Life. This is the actual receiving of Eternal Life, the nature of God.

When you receive this nature you lose the old Satanic nature.

You cannot have the two natures at the same time. If you did, you would belong to two families at the same time.

God would be your Father, and Satan would be your father. When you died, you would have to go to both heaven and hell.

The part of man that is recreated is his spirit. His intellect is renewed. His body is healed—if sick.

I want you to see clearly that this New Creation created in Christ Jesus, who has become a partaker of the Divine Nature, has passed out of Satanic dominion into the dominion of Jesus Christ.

Jesus is the Lord over this New Creation.

Gal. 6:15, "For neither is circumcision anything, nor uncircumcision, but a new creation."

Eph. 2:8-9, "For by grace have ye been saved through faith; and that not of yourselves, it is the gift of God; not of works, that no man should glory."

All that an unsaved man does in repenting, in giving up sin, in penance, is the work of an unregenerate man. It has no standing with God.

God takes the sinner as he is. No matter how deep in sin he has gone the New Birth will straighten him out.

We have thought that a sinner could pray through, that he could repent until God would forgive him.

All that is unscriptural.

It is all right for a Jew under the Law, but not for a sinner under grace.

The sinner is dead. He is sin. All the good works that he does are the works of sin. God does not want them.

God takes him as he is—full of sin, rebellion, Satanic nature—and imparts to him His nature.

His nature drives out that foul, unclean nature of Satan and makes him a New Creation. All the sins of that Old Creation are remitted instantaneously.

The man stands before the Father as though sin had never been.

The next step in the drama is the crux of the whole thing.

2 Cor. 5:21, "Him who knew no sin God made to be sin on

our behalf; that we might become the righteousness of God in him."

Everything we have done so far has been to one end, that man might become the righteousness of God in Christ.

What does Righteousness mean?

It is the ability to stand in the Father's presence as though sin had never been, as free as Adam was before he transgressed.

John 8:36, "If therefore the Son shall make you free, ye shall be free indeed (or in reality)."

In the New Creation the Son has made us free.

Rom. 8:1, "There is therefore now no condemnation to them that are in Christ Jesus.".

We are New Creations. We are the Righteousness of God in Christ. We have arrived; We are children of God.

The only righteousness the church has known has been the Calvanistic type that made an unworthy man righteous.

The new kind of Righteousness, that Paul described, is the Righteousness of a righteous man whom God has made good by imparting his very nature to him.

When He said my righteous ones shall live by Faith, He is describing a New Creation that has been made righteous with His own nature.

This is not a legal righteousness, nor a reckoned righteousness, but the actual impartation of God's own righteous nature.

Chapter VIII

RIGHTEOUSNESS RESTORED

UNIVERSAL Sin Consciousness is the parent of all the religions of the earth.

Man has ever sought to rid himself of the sense of guilt and sin. , Sin Consciousness was born at the Fall. It was manifested in Adam's fear to meet God and his desire to cover his nakedness.

The Revelation of God and the development of that Revelation have been to one end—to restore Righteousness to man.

The meaning of Righteousness in this sense is the ability to stand in the presence of God without the sense of sin, guilt, or inferiority. It also includes the legal relation of a son, and fellowship with the Father God.

When Adam sinned he instantly lost fellowship with Jehovah and the ability to approach Him.

This Sin Consciousness has robbed man of his faith and filled him with a sense of unworthiness that dominates human consciousness today.

Now the problem is this: Has God provided a Redemption that will take away this Sin Consciousness and permit man to come into His presence now and stand there as Jesus did?

If God could do that, then faith is restored, for the great enemy of faith is the sense of unworthiness.

Theology has failed to interpret the plan of Redemption in such a manner as to remove this Sin Consciousness from the minds of those who accept Christ.

In fact, most of the ministers who are classed among the orthodox, continually preach sin instead of Righteousness, and keep their congregations under condemnation rather than lead them out into liberty where faith can function.

I have come to see that the basis of real faith is to let the Christian know that Righteousness has been restored to him.

In Job 33:26 is a prophecy that is very striking. It is a picture of the New Birth.

I can give you only one verse: "He prayeth unto God, and he is favorable unto him, So that he seeth his face with joy: And he restoreth unto man his righteousness."

There are three facts here.

First, man prays and God hears his prayer.

Second, "He seeth his face with joy"—restored fellowship.

Third, "He restoreth unto man his righteousness."

In these three statements we have the result of a complete Redemption.

In another chapter I am going to show you the different

types of Righteousness that have been granted to man down through the ages, until God in Christ restored this perfect, God satisfying Righteousness to us.

The book of Romans is a story of how God restored Righteousness to us on the ground of faith in Jesus Christ. It is the great master-drama of humanity.

In Rom. 1:16-17, Paul declares: "For I am not ashamed of the gospel of Christ: for it is the power of God unto salvation to every one that believeth; to the Jew first, and also to the Greek. For therein (in this gospel) is revealed a righteousness of God from faith unto faith: as it is written, But the righteous shall live by faith."

This Righteousness that is revealed is the Righteousness that the believer receives in Christ.

In the first three chapters, up to the eighteenth verse of the third chapter, we have God showing how the Jew and the Gentile both have utterly failed to attain a Righteousness that would give them a standing with God.

He concludes the argument in Rom. 3:9-18 with fourteen charges in the grand indictment against man.

In the first charge He says, "There is none righteous, no, not one."

No man has a standing with God outside of Christ.

These fourteen charges are laid against the unregenerate man, not the Christian.

In the 19th and 20th verses He sums up the case. He shows that the Gentiles without law failed, and the Jews under the law have failed to attain Righteousness before God.

Then in Rom. 3:21-26 we get God's statement of how this Righteousness has been restored to man upon legal grounds.

"But now apart from the law a righteousness of God hath been manifested, being witnessed by the law and the prophets." Another translation is, "A Righteousness has come to light."

Did you notice the expression "apart from the law"?

Independent of the law a Righteousness of God hath been manifested, and the law witnesses to its validity as well as the prophets.

He says, "Even the righteousness (not "a" righteousness, but "the" righteousness) of God through faith in Jesus Christ unto all them that believe; for there is no distinction; for all have sinned and fall short of the glory of God; being justified freely by his grace through the redemption that is in Christ Jesus."

Rom. 3:26, "For the showing, I say, of his righteousness at this present season: that he might himself be righteous and the righteousness of him that hath faith in Jesus." (Mar. Am. Rev.)

God is not afraid to become the Righteousness of the man who has faith in Jesus because He planned that Redemption.

It is faith in His own Son and what that Son has wrought for man.

God is not ashamed to become the Righteousness of the New Creation. If there is anything that ought to free us and lift us above the age-old master, Sin Consciousness, it is this fact.

In I Cor. 1:30, Jesus is declared to be our Righteousness.

"But of him are ye in Christ Jesus, who was made unto us wisdom from God, and righteousness, and sanctification, and redemption."

Here God declares He is our Righteousness.

And in 2 Cor. 5:21, by the New Birth He makes us His Righteousness in Christ.

No man who has received Eternal Life and given his spirit an opportunity to develop by feeding on the Word can ever challenge his standing with the Father.

Never again will he shrink under that sin teaching of the modern pulpit and look upon himself as a failure and sin-ruled.

He is a master. He has as much a right before the throne of grace as Jesus has upon it. He has as much a right in the Father's presence as the Father has a right to sit upon His own throne.

Why? Because the Father Himself planned the Redemption and wrought the Redemption through His Son, and sets His seal upon that Redemptive work by making the believer in Jesus Christ Righteous with His own Righteousness.

Chapter IX

REDISCOVERY OF PAUL'S EPISTLES

HERE is a new interest in the Epistles.

Paul's Epistles are a revelation of the two-fold unveiling of Redemption—the legal and the vital side of that mighty plan.

They give us the answer to Job 33:26 (American Revision). "And he restoreth unto man his righteousness".

The Recovery of Righteousness

It is a legal recovery.

The definition of Righteousness as seen in the Pauline Revelation is the ability to stand in God's presence without the sense of guilt or inferiority.

The great major theme of these Epistles is the new Righteousness in contrast to the old Righteousness under the Law.

One is by grace, the other by works. One was a limited Righteousness, the other an unlimited Righteousness. One gave man the standing of a servant, the other the standing of a son.

This new kind of Righteousness was the "mystery kept hidden through the ages". It was revealed by God to man through Paul.

It is the revelation of a new kind of Fellowship based upon legal grounds.

Man lost his Fellowship in the Garden. It had never been restored to him.

Fellowship is the ultimate of God's dream for man.

I Cor. 1:9 "God is faithful, through whom ye were called into the fellowship of his Son Jesus Christ our Lord."

Our Fellowship is with the Father and with the Son.

The New Kind of Love

It is the revelation of a new kind of love.

Natural, human love has failed. It is the tragedy of the human race. Love is the best thing that natural man has, but it turns to jealousy, bitter hatred, and sometimes murder.

The new kind of love is never selfish, never seeks its own. It comes from the heart of the Father God who is love.

This new kind of love is the greatest thing that ever came to man. It is the solution of the human problem.

It is not only a revelation of these mighty things, but it is also a revelation of the new kind of Life.

Jesus said, "I am come that ye might have life."

The New Creation is receiving the nature and life of God.

It makes man God's son, makes man one with Christ and one with the Father.

It is the outstanding feature of Christianity—the greatest miracle of the ages.

A New Covenant

It is the revelation of a New Covenant.

The Old Covenant with its offerings, sacrifices, and laws was fulfilled and set aside.

The New Covenant was instituted with the sacrifice of Jesus Christ. He became the High Priest, and we became the priests of this New Covenant.

It is the Covenant that binds the believer to Christ, and Christ to the Believer—Jesus himself being the security.

It is the advent of a new wisdom.

Christ was made unto us wisdom. It is the wisdom that cometh down from above.

This wisdom that cometh down from above is the ability to understand Revelation Knowledge.

Wisdom is the fruit of the human spirit. This new kind of wisdom is the fruit of the recreated and indwelt human spirit.

It is the revelation of the Lordship of Jesus—as well as the lordship of love and the lordship of the Word.

They all mean practically the same thing.

It is the revelation of a new kind of faith, of a faith walk, of a faith life.

Christianity is called "The Faith".

It is the revelation of the present ministry of Christ at the right hand of the Father.

It is the revelation of the Church as the body of Christ.

It is the revelation of the work of Christ from the Cross to the Throne.

A Revelation of His present ministry at the Right Hand of God for the Believer.

Chapter X

TRUE CONCEPTION OF GOD

IN Consciousness has given us a wrong picture of God and a wrong picture of the New Creation.

It has made us see God as a holy, just, austere, and unapproachable Being who is ever on the alert to discover sin in us and condemn us.

That conception has made us afraid and caused us to shrink from Him.

The conception is wrong: He is a Father God.

John 14.23 says that He will make His home with us.

"If a man love me, he will keep my word: and my Father will love him, and we will come unto him, and make our abode with him."

John 16:27, "For the Father himself loveth you."

John 17:23, "That the world may know that thou didst send me, and lovedst them, even as thou lovedst me."

This is a complete repudiation of the modern theological view of the Father God.

When we know Him as a loving, tender Father who longs for our fellowship and longs to live with us, the whole picture is changed.

Relationship teaching has never been given its place.

We have never thought of ourselves as the very sons and daughters of God.

Most of the hymns written on this subject tell us that we are adopted into the family of God.

We know that an adopted child is not a real child and never can be.

The child of God is not only recreated and born of the Spirit of God, but he is also legally adopted.

Romans 8:15, "For ye received not the spirit of bondage again unto fear; but ye received the spirit of adoption, whereby we cry, Abba, Father."

He has a double relationship—a legal relationship and a vital relationship with the Father God.

The New Creation fact has never been brought to the front.

The Word declares that we are New Creations, that the old things connected with the "fallen nature" are passed away. The old things of doubt, fear, and bondage to sickness and want have passed away.

Romans 6:5-11, "For if we have become united with him in the likeness of his death, we shall be also in the likeness (or united with) of His resurrection; knowing this, that our old man was crucified with him, that the body of sin might be done away, that so we should no longer be in bondage to sin; for he that hath died is justified from sin. But if we died with Christ, we believe that we shall also live with him; knowing that Christ being raised from the dead dieth no more; death no more hath dominion over him. For the death that he died, he died unto sin once: but the life that he liveth, he liveth unto God. Even so reckon ye also yourselves to be dead unto sin, but alive unto God in Christ Jesus."

The New Creation is complete in Christ, perfectly cared for, perfectly loved.

In the presence of such great Scriptures, as 2 Cor. 5:21, we should repudiate every thought of weakness and Sin Consciousness, rise to the level of our place in Christ, and declare our freedom.

"Him who knew no sin he made to be sin on our behalf; that we might become the righteousness of God in Him."

We have become the Righteousness of God in Him, but we have been living as slaves when we ought to reign as kings. We yielded without a fight when we heard the Adversary roar about our unworthiness to stand in God's presence.

Everytime we confess our weakness, we repudiate the finished work of Christ and belittle our own position and standing in Christ.

Phil. 4:13, "I can do all things in him that strengtheneth me."

The mind must be fully satisfied with the evidence of a New Creation, a Redemption from Satan's dominion, and an emancipation from sin.

This can only come to us through the Word.

The Scriptures in this study absolutely settle that issue.

The sin problem stops being a problem the moment we know what we are in Christ.

Faith is a problem only to those who are ignorant of their rights and privileges, and their place in Christ.

Heb. 1:3-4 tells us that when Christ had made the great substitution, He sat down at the right hand of the Majesty on High.

"Who being the effulgence of his glory, and the very image of his substance, and upholding all things by the word of his power, when he had made purification of sins, sat down on the right hand of the Majesty on high; having become by so much better than the angels, as he hath inherited a more excellent name than they."

He could not have been accepted by the Father and been given that seat at the Father's right hand unless He had made possible the New Creation, a perfect fellowship, and a perfect standing with the Father for all who believe on Him.

Heb. 9:11-12 tells us that Christ carried His blood into the Heavenly Holy of Holies and made an eternal Redemption.

"But Christ having come a high priest of the good things to come, through the greater and more perfect tabernacle, not made with hands, that is to say, not of this creation, nor yet through the blood of goats and calves, but with his own blood, entered in once for all into the holy place, having obtained eternal redemption."

If that is done then our Redemption is a complete, finished thing.

God declares that it is.

Satan's dominion over us is broken.

Heb. 9:24-26 declares that He is in the Father's presence on our behalf, after putting sin away by the sacrifice of Himself.

Heb. 7:25, "Wherefore also he is able to save to the uttermost them that draw near unto God through him, seeing he ever liveth to make intercession for them."

The word "save" also means "heal";

In His mind there are no incurables.

He climaxes the whole thing by declaring that He made one sacrifice for sins forever, so that the man who accepts Him as his Saviour becomes God's child.

As His child, man becomes the Righteousness of God in Christ.

Now we can approach the Father at any time or anywhere with a quiet certainty that we have an audience.

Faith has ceased to be a problem. Sin has ceased to be a problem.

Righteousness has ceased to be a problem. Sonship has ceased to be a problem.

We are now in Christ, New Creations, children of God.

1 John 3:2, "Beloved, now are we children of God."

We are not problem children. We are children endowed with His ability, children beloved of the Father.

Chapter XI

FELLOWSHIP THROUGH RIGHTEOUSNESS

COR. 1:9 "God is faithful, through whom ye were call- ed into the fellowship of His Son Jesus Christ our Lord."

Do you think the Father would call us into fellowship with His Son if we were not righteous?

Do you think John could write 1 John 1:1-4 under the di- rection of the Holy Spirit if we were not righteous?

"That which was from the beginning (that means the Incarnation), that which we have heard, that which we have seen with our eyes, that which we beheld, and our hands han- dled, concerning the Word of life (and the life was manifested, and we have seen, and bear witness, and declare unto you the life, the eternal life, which was with the Father, and was mani- fested unto us)."

That Eternal Life was Jesus. Now we can understand what it means.

"He that hath the Son hath the Life."

Jesus is that Eternal Life which was manifested.

Notice the next two verses. "That which we have seen and heard declare we unto you."

Why?

"That ye also may have fellowship with us: yea, and our fellowship is with the Father, and with his Son Jesus Christ."

We are not only called into fellowship with the Son, but we are also called into fellowship with the Father.

The Word "fellowship" is translated from the Greek word which is translated "communion" in some places.

Communion and fellowship are identical. They mean bliss- ful harmony. They mean that our spirits and the Holy Spirit through the Word, are in perfect accord.

Now we are assuming the positions of sons. We are bear- ing the burdens of the Master in His stead. We are fellow- shipping Him. We are taking over His burdens.

Our fellowship is manifold. We have fellowship with the Father. We have fellowship with the Son. We have fellowship with the Holy Spirit. We have fellowship with the Word. And we also have fellowship with each other.

The most vital, and the one that means the most to us, is our fellowship with the Word.

We have this Revelation from the heart of the Father to feed upon.

Matt. 4:4, "Man shall not live by bread alone, but by every word that proceedeth out of the mouth of God."

Daily, we feed and meditate upon the Word until men and women feel the presence and power of the Unseen One in our lives.

We face life's problems fearlessly.

Rev. 12:11, "And they overcame him because of the blood of the Lamb, and because of the word of their testimony."

The Word here is "Logos". It is Jesus.

They overcame him by the Word that was in their lips.

Broken Fellowship

He tells us in 1 John 1:6, "If we say that we have fellowship with him and walk in the darkness, we lie, and do not the truth: but if we walk in the light, as he is in the light, we have fellowship one with another, and the blood of Jesus his Son cleanseth us from all sin."

The thing that makes the church the most beautiful place in the world is not the building. It is the people who are in fellowship with one another and with the Lord Jesus.

The moment we sin against our brother, we break fellowship with Him. When we break fellowship with Him we go into darkness and there is no getting out of that darkness until we confess our sins.

I John 1:9, "If we confess our sins, he is faithful and righteous to forgive us our sins, and to cleanse us from all unrighteousness."

When we confess our sin to the Father, He is faithful and righteous to forgive us.

If a man should say, "I have no fellowship with the Father —somehow or other I have lost it and yet I have not committed sin", the man is ignorant or else he is lying because the Father does not withdraw His fellowship unless we have sinned.

"If we say we have not sinned, we deceive ourselves, and the truth is not in us."

This has reference to broken fellowship.

No man needs to stay in broken fellowship. Acting on 1 John 1:9 restores righteousness to him.

No human religion, no philosophy, no works that natural man can do will ever give him fellowship with the Father or Righteousness which makes it possible for him to stand in the Father's presence without Sin Consciousness.

In other words, no man can have fellowship with the Father and be free from Sin Consciousness until he is a New Creation, until he becomes the Righteousness of God in Christ. But the instant a man is Born Again, he becomes the Righteousness of God in Christ.

Then he has fellowship with the Father. He can stand in the Father's presence as though he had never sinned.

The Church His Body Possessing Righteousness

Eph. 1:4, "Even as he chose us in him before the foundation of the world, that we should be holy and without blemish before him: in love having marked us out for the position of sons." (Literal Translation).

This is God's declaration that, in this present life, He planned we should be holy and without blemish before Him. This is not after we die, but today.

That holiness and beauty of life is all of grace, not of ourselves. The only thing we do is receive it, accept it with joy.

Eph. 5:25 speaking of Christ and the church, and using marriage as an illustration says, "Husbands, love your wives, even as Christ also loved the church, and gave himself up for it; that he might sanctify it, having cleansed it by the washing of water with the word, that he might present the church to himself a glorious church, not having spot or wrinkle or any such thing; but that it should be holy and without blemish."

He does not say that the church is going to be a conqueror after it gets to heaven, but that it is a conqueror now.

It is not going to be sanctified after it gets to heaven but now.

It is not going to be cleansed by the washing of the Word after it gets to heaven but now.

The Word is the thing that brings knowledge.

The ignorance of the church about the Bible is appalling. It is because of textual preaching.

The exposition of the Word makes men spiritual. It makes them hungry for the Word so that they study the Word for themselves.

This church "without spot or wrinkle" is the church that has been cleansed through the Word of God.

It is not cleansed by prayer only but by the Word. It is the Spirit that uses the Word to build the life of Christ into us.

Col. 1:21-22 gives us another picture of the church.

"And you, being in time past alienated and enemies in your mind in your evil works, yet now hath he reconciled in the body of his flesh through death, to present you holy and without blemish and unreprovable before him."

This is a beautiful picture of the recreated body—reconciled, holy, without blemish, without reproof, standing before the Father, not only clothed in the Righteousness of Christ but actually partakers of His Righteousness. This is a photo of our present walk in Christ.

Eph. 4:23-24, "That ye be renewed in the spirit of your mind, and put on the new man, that after God hath been created in righteousness and holiness of truth."

This New Creation is created out of Righteousness.

Righteousness is the nature of the Father God. We have partaken of that Righteousness—that nature of God.

We are to put on the conduct of the new man in our daily life. We are no longer to talk like the old man.

The old man lived in failure, in selfishness, in greed, in fear.

The new man lives in the fulness of love. He is Jesus-like —dominated by heaven and heaven's sweet spirit.

The old creation and the new are as far apart as God and Satan.

Heb. 13:20-21, "Now the God of peace, who brought again from the dead the great shepherd of the sheep with the blood of an eternal covenant, even our Lord Jesus, make you perfect in every good thing to do his will, working in us that which is well pleasing in his sight."

It is the purpose of the risen Christ to "make us perfect in every good thing to do His will."

It is His business to work in us His own good pleasure, making us beautiful in the sight of the Father.

Phil. 1:6 carries us a step farther in this.

"Being confident of this very thing, that he who began a good work in you will perfect it until the day of Jesus Christ."

He has begun His good work. He started it at the New Birth. Now He is taking the things of Jesus and building them into us.

The very life of Christ is being built into us. This is done by our living in the Word and the Word dominating our daily walk.

The love nature must gain the ascendency in us until our words are soaked in love, until our whole spirit is held in a solution as it were of the love nature of the Father.

Phil. 2:13 becomes a glorious reality.

"For it is God who is at work within you, willing and working his own good pleasure."

It is God reproducing Himself in us. We are to live and walk and talk in love.

1 Pet. 5:10 has another sweet message for our hearts.

"And the God of all grace, who called you unto his eternal glory in Christ, after that ye have suffered a little while, shall himself perfect, establish, strengthen you."

We may be going through hard places. We may be suffering. There may not be much happiness for us in this life, but there can be joy.

Happiness comes from our surroundings; joy comes from our recreated hearts.

We have Him in our hearts. He will strengthen us, establish us, until our lives become like Jesus' life.

Eph. 5:1-2, "Be ye therefore imitators of God, as beloved children (or children of love)."

What would we do if we imitated God?

We would love

"And walk in love, even as Christ also loved you, and gave himself up for you."

We are to give ourselves up as an odor, a sweet, fragrant offering of love to the world. They may criticize and hate us, but we love them.

We walk in love toward them. Until we love as He loves, we do not represent Him.

He never answered back. He never said unkind things. He never criticized. He never peddled scandal. He spoke love words. He helped men and women. He said beautiful things.

This walking in love is the most beautiful thing in the world. God is love. We are born of love. Love is the rule and law of our life. Love is the strength of our life. Love is the very beauty of our life. We are walking as He walked.

This is the Righteousness of God in us. It is in reality our life in Christ.

1 John 4:17, "Herein is love made perfect with us, that we may have boldness in the day of judgment; because as He is, even so are we in this world.

We are here as He is up there.

1 John 4:18, "There is no fear in love: but perfect love casteth out fear."

There is no fear in love. We are living in love. We have come to believe in love.

We know that He is love. We know that we are abiding in love. We know that love is abiding in us.

This is the secret of faith.

This Revelation to Paul and John is a series of pictures of us that our Father has put in His album.

We are finding ourselves complete in Him.

Col. 2:9-10, "For in him dwelleth all the fulness of the Godhead bodily, and in him ye are made full, who is the head of all principality and power."

That is how we appear to our Father. That is the way love sees us, even as it saw Him.

It sees us as New Love Creations, ruled by love, living in love, and letting love live in us.

All this is possible. All this is ours.

Chapter XII

RIGHTEOUSNESS BY FAITH

THE church does not appreciate what she is as declared in the Word.

We have been taught that we were unworthy and unrighteous, that we were weak and had no faith, for so long that it has become a chronic disease. We look with fear upon any message that brings relief unless it is a message of works.

If we could sacrifice something, if we could pray long enough and hard enough, if we could confess our sins enough, then in some way we might get straightened out in our spiritual life.

The whole thing is wrong.

Righteousness comes by faith. It is not gained by works, by repentance, by crying or by weeping. Neither does it come by the way of begging.

It comes only by the way of faith.

Man has alwas sought to get Righteousness by works. If we thought we could become the Righteousness of God by praying for a certain number of hours, we would do it.

If we were told that someone had obtained Righteousness by confessing all their sins since childhood and by making restitution for them, we would be willing to make the effort.

Righteousness does not come that way.

It comes by faith. Not by your work but by Christ's work. Not by your tears but by the tears of Christ.

If everyone of us knew that we have Righteousness in us, we would become entirely independent of circumstances.

If we were as conscious of being the Righteousness of God as we are conscious of being weak and unworthy, we would not be sick any longer, we would not be held in bondage to want and poverty.

If we were as conscious of our Identification with Jesus Christ and our oneness with Him as we are conscious of physical pain and physical need, we would never have pain and we would never mention our needs again.

This new sense of Righteousness, this new fact of Righteousness, this new discovery of our being the Righteousness of God in Christ gives us a new sense of freedom in Christ.

It utterly destroys the Sin Consciousness and the Weakness Consciousness and the Want Consciousness. In their place has come the all absorbing reality of Christ.

We know that He is our Righteousness and that we are the Righteousness of God in Him.

He is with us in all His ability and strength, in all His completeness and fulness. We are not afraid of circumstances.

He whispers, "Fear thou not, for I am with thee; be not dismayed, for I am thy God; I will strengthen thee; yea, I will help thee; yea, I will uphold thee with the right hand of my righteousness."

He is with us. He is the God of the New Creation.

He is our strength. He is upholding us with His Righteousness.

We cannot fail. We cannot be kept in bondage.

This gives us a new liberty in prayer, a new sense of authority as sons and daughters of God to use the Name of Jesus, a new joy in fellowship with the Father.

There is a new freshness in the Word. It has become literally His Word to us.

Its absoluteness grips our hearts.

We may not have realized it before but the Father and Jesus are speaking to us.

The Word is the voice of the Father. He is not speaking to multitudes. He is speaking to each one of us.

He declares that we have become the Righteousness of God in Him. We know that we are what He declares us to be.

Then there comes a new sense of mastery. We are coming into our rights, our legal rights in Christ.

Our steps are sure now. No longer is there any uncertainty.

We are not afraid of what the day may bring forth.

We know what it means when He says, "Greater is he that is in you than he that is in the world."

We know what it means when He says, "Ye are of God, my little children, and have overcome them."

He is talking to us.

The sense of mastery, the strange new dignity of sonship, sweeps over our hearts.

We understand what it means to be under orders from heaven.

We are ambassadors. We are clothed with authority from heaven.

Luke 24:49, "But tarry ye in the city, until ye be clothed with ability from on high."

Now we understand what Jesus meant when He said that demons and the forces of darkness would be subject to us.

Weakness, fear of failure—the little kingdoms that once ruled the world have been subordinated by Jesus Christ.

Jesus conquered Satan. Every Satan-ruled force is subject to His Name.

He put Satan and all his works under our feet.

Now we know what Redemption means. We know we have become "the fulness of Him that filleth all in all."

We know that "of His fulness have we all received and grace upon grace."

We know that we have received "the abundance of grace and the gift of righteousness."

We reign as kings in the realm of life through Jesus Christ.

We begin to understand I Cor. 12:3, "And no man can say, Jesus is Lord, but in the Holy Spirit."

Now we say it as New Creations conscious of our standing and our rights.

Satan's dominion has been broken.

The Lordship of Jesus has begun.

We shall not want because we are one with Him. He is the Vine, we are the branches. We are the fruit bearing portion of the Vine.

We are His lips! We are His hands!

We are living with Him. He is living in us—unseen but real.

We walk with Him.

All this Righteousness gives us.

Chapter XIII

RIGHTEOUSNESS UNDER THE COVENANTS

T thrilled me when I realized what mighty achievements were wrought by men who had only limited Righteousness under the First Covenant.

I thought of Abraham. As soon as he was circumcized and came into the Covenant, God gave him a limited Righteousness.

I thought of his daring to stand in the presence of God and plead for Sodom and Gomorrah with that lofty fearlessness that is not matched in our modern day by men who know their unlimited Righteousness and rights in Christ.

I thought of the mighty acts of Moses who only had a servant's place before Jehovah, yet he dared to obey God and achieved such marvelous victories for that slave nation, Israel.

I thought of Joshua who dared to obey Jehovah and led that nation down to the shore of the Jordan when it was at flood-tide. He dared to say to the priests, "Take the Ark and go down and dip your feet into the water, and when you do a way will be opened for you to go through dry shod." And yet, this man Joshua had only limited Righteousness—the Righteousness of a servant.

We see him stand before the armies and cry to the sun, "Stand still until the nation is avenged of its enemies."

That man dominated the universe, and yet he had but limited Righteousness.

We see Elijah at the Battle of the Gods on Mount Carmel calling down fire out of heaven, bringing rain upon a drought stricken land.

He was an absolute master of the laws of nature. And yet, he was but a servant with a servant's standing and a servant's limited Righteousness.

Space will not allow us to speak of Daniel and the three Hebrew children, or of David's mighty men of war.

They had only limited Righteousness, yet what prodigies they wrought.

Their Righteousness was reckoned to them on the ground of the value that God placed upon the blood of bulls and goats, upon the sacredness of His Covenant with Abraham.

They were not Recreated men and women as we are.

They were but servants under a law that must be set aside for another to take its place, which was to be based upon a better sacrifice and better blood.

Our hearts thrilled as we read of their obedience to the command of an Angel.

44

They did not walk by faith as we do. They walked by sight. They saw the Angel. They heard his voice.

They lived in the realm of the Senses.

Their outstanding characteristic was obedience to the voice of God.

He has given us a record of their mighty achievements based upon their obedience to the Abrahamic Covenant.

Unlimited Righteousness

I once craved to get God's estimation of our Righteousness, of our standing before the Father, and of our rights and privileges in Christ; in the New Covenant.

I found it in the Pauline Revelation. I saw what we were in the mind of the Father and in the mind of the Master. I saw our limitless possibilities in the New Covenant and in our relation to Him as sons and daughters.

Jesus was the "sample" Son.

He said, "Greater works than these shall ye do because I go unto the Father."

Then He gave us a legal right to the use of His Name, and finally in the Great Commission He defines the ability of that Name.

He said, "In my name, ye shall cast out demons."

When He declared that, He let us into the secret that we were to be masters of Satan.

For if we can cast out one demon, we can cast out all demons. If we have dominion over the Adversary, we have dominion over all His works.

Do you see the limitlessness of this Righteousness that permits us to stand in the Father's presence without the sense of guilt or condemnation, and gives us the ability to stand in the presence of Satan without the sense of inferiority?

When He said, "All authority hath been given unto me in heaven and on earth,"—that was for the church, that was for this dispensation.

That authority was not for Jesus but for us.

His Name made us free from condemnation, free from Satanic dominion, by His redemption and by our New Creation.

On the basis of that He calls us to do the things that Jesus began to do—set men free, break the bonds of Satan over men and women, heal the sick, break the power of demons over communities and nations.

When He said, "All authority hath been given unto me in heaven and on earth. Go ye therefore, and make disciples of all nations, baptizing them in the name of the Father and of the Son and of the Holy Spirit: teaching them to observe all things whatsoever I commanded you," you notice they were taken into the school of Christ and taught the possibilities of all our rights and privileges in Christ, our complete Redemption from Satan, and our dominion over him.

Then He said, "And lo, I am with you always, even unto the end of the age."

I began to understand the Commission.

He said, "In my name shall they cast out demons." And also, "Whatsoever ye shall ask in my name, that will I do, that the Father may be glorified in the Son."

We can see very clearly now that we are to take Jesus' place and act within the authority that has been invested in His Name.

That authority belongs to us.

We can see another fact. When Adam was created, God gave him dominion over all the works of His hands, but Adam turned that dominion over into the hands of Satan and became the subject of Satan.

In Christ that Dominion is restored to the Church. It is restored in the Name of Jesus. That lost authority was invested in Christ.

When He said, "All authority hath been given unto me in heaven and on earth. Go ye therefore and use this authority. I will give you the legal right to the use of my Name. I will give you the Power of Attorney," He bids us to come boldly to the throne room, to the throne of grace, and make our requests known.

We are not to come there as slaves or as servants.

We come as sons. We are the love slaves of that master love slave—Jesus.

We are acting in His stead. We are taking His place. We are doing the work that He came to do. We are acting with an unlimited Righteousness. We are taking our place and using to the full our rights in Christ.

The church has had a wrong conception of its place in Christ and of its dominion.

We have been filled with fear. We have heard so much preaching about sin and weakness and failure that it has become a part of our very consciousness.

We have not realized what He said, "Ye are of God, my little children, and have overcome them: because greater is he that is in you than he that is in the world."

Who is it that is in us? God.

We are masters. We are overcomers.

In the next chapter, 1 John 5:4-5, He said, "Whatsoever is begotten of God overcometh the world: and this is the victory that hath overcome the world, even our faith. And who is he that overcometh the world, but he that believeth that Jesus is the Son of God?"

46

We are masters in the mind of the Father.

We are overcomers.

The moment we get that mental attitude of victors, instead of being conquered, we are going to take our place.

He climaxes the Paulines Revelation in Rom. 8:37.

"Nay, in all these things we are more than conquerors through him that loved us."

He makes us see in Rom. 5:17 that we reign as kings in the realm of life through Jesus Christ.

Of His fulness have we received and grace upon grace to enjoy that measure of fulness.

He has put all things in subjection under our feet.

He gave Jesus, our Lord, to be Head over all the governments of the world.

We are to function as rulers that dominate spiritual forces and reign as kings on earth now in Jesus Christ.

Understand that he who can rule spiritual forces can also rule political conditions. The church should absolutely dominate the political elements of the world for the benefit of the human race.

We have unlimited Righteousness.

Let us take our limitless privileges and act the part of God's own rulers in this world of darkness and hatred and selfishness.

What Limits Our Using Our Righteousness

What is it that limits our acting upon the Word and taking our place in Christ? What is it that holds us from taking advantage of our Righteousness in Christ?

We know that we are the Righteousness of God in Christ. We know that God is the strength of our lives. We know that we have His ability. We know that He is our sufficiency to meet every crisis in our lives. We know that His Word in our lips will heal the sick, strengthen the weak, awaken the unsaved to their condition and bring them to a saving knowledge of Christ.

All this we know. Why are we so slow to act?

It may be an unrenewed mind.

After one is Born Again and comes into this vast inheritance of Grace, his mind is not in harmony with his recreated spirit. So, it is necessary that his mind be renewed.

This unrenewed mind holds many men and women, who might be greatly used of the Lord, in a state of uselessness.

Their minds may be renewed by acting on the Word, and by an intimate acquaintance with the Master through the Word.

When the Word is ignored, reason takes the throne.

Another reason why men fail to use their Righteousness is

because the Senses rule their spirits. Fear and unbelief are on the throne. They are afraid to take their place.

They see the need. They know they should be able to set that person free who is held in bondage by the Adversary, but that unrenewed mind, that lack of spiritual initiative, benumbs them.

This comes from a low type of fellowship with the Father.

They have no real appetite for the Word. They enjoy reading about the Bible more than they enjoy feasting upon it.

Lordship of the Word

There is no sense of appreciation of the Lordship of the Word, of its authority in their lips, or of their ability through the Word to stir men and women to real action.

If one lacks the sense of the Lordship of the Word, they will never be able to use it although they may intellectually know that they are the Righteousness of God, that they have the ability of God, that they have a legal right to the use of Jesus' Name with all its authority.

This comes from a low type of fellowship, from walking out of love.

They do not recognize the Lordship of love nor the Lordship of the Word. They have no fearless confession of what they are in Christ.

There is a sense of feebleness of spirit, a vacillating faith, a yielding to circumstances.

All the time they will acknowledge that they are the Righteousness of God, yet they are not taking advantage of it.

They are living in bondage to the Senses.

They are not practising the Word of Righteousness.

They are unconsciously turning to the Senses for help and succour in their hour of need.

They act like common men. They are moved by the jealousies of those around them. They ignore their place in Christ.

In a time of crisis they seek for someone else to pray for them or to act for them.

They ignore the use of the Name of Jesus. They forget what manner of men they are.

They are living mediocre lives when they should be Super-Men.

They are weak when they should be strong.

They have everything. They know their wealth. They know their rights. And yet they live in spiritual poverty.

Why? Because they are not taking their place and acting on the Word.

Chapter XIV

RIGHTEOUSNESS MAKES US MASTERS OF EVIL

F we can enter the Throne Room without fear, if we can stand in His presence without fear, then we know that we are His Righteousness in Christ and that we are masters of all evil.

Satan and demons knew Jesus. They knew who He was, and they knew what He was. They knew also that Jesus was aware of who He was.

Satan and demons know who we are, but ofttimes we ourselves do not know.

Jesus said, "I came out from the Father."

We can say, "We know we are born of God and that whosoever is born of God overcometh the world."

Have you ever realized what it means to come boldly to the throne of grace?

Have you ever realized what it means for us to be able to stand in the Father's presence today as Jesus did in His earth walk?

Do you know that we have as much a right to be free from Sin Consciousness as Jesus was in His earthly ministry?

If we can stand in the presence of the Father without the sense of inferiority or sin, we are masters of every force and power of hell.

Satan is defeated.

When we know we are His Righteousness and know it as Jesus knew who He was, we will not fear evil, we will not fear any disease, we will not fear the lack of money. We will know we are absolute masters over every power of the Enemy.

We will know that Phil. 4:19 is ours.

"And my God shall supply every need of yours according to his riches in glory in Christ Jesus."

There will be no worry about our finances. We will simply call His attention to our needs and they will be met.

Jesus said, "Your Heavenly Father knoweth that ye have need of all these things. But seek ye first his kingdom and his righteousness; and all these things shall be added unto you."

We have sought His Righteousness and have found it. We have become His Righteousness in Christ.

Righteousness means the ability to stand in the Father's presence as though sin had never touched us, with the same liberty and freedom that Jesus had with the Father in His earth walk.

When we confess the Lordship of Jesus, it is not only His

Lordship over us but it is His Lordship over all evil through us and by us.

The moment we make this confession, we are one with Him. We are His representatives in the earth.

We are acting in the Name of Jesus.

In His Name we are masters. In His Name we are conquerors. In His Name we dominate circumstances and evil forces.

When we recognize His Lordship over us, it is His Lordship through us. It is His Lordship in our words, so we can say, "In Jesus Name, demon, leave that body."

We can say to that disease, "T.B. in the Name of Jesus Christ, your Master, leave that body", and it will leave.

We are masters because He is our Master. And as our Master, He is working through us.

He is lording it over the forces of darkness through us.

We have become His Righteousness by receiving Eternal Life, the very nature of the Father.

The moment that becomes a reality to us, we become overcomers. Demons will fear us even as they feared Jesus.

How many times they must have said, "If that man knew his authority, he would send us off into the abyss". But he did not know his authority!

He was praying for faith. He was trying to get power. He was fasting and crying and pleading with God to give him something that he already possessed.

He had the authority. He had the ability to use that authority. But he did not know it!

We have become as He was in His earth walk. He became as we were to the end that we might become as He was, and now is.

By the New Creation we are branches of the Vine, members of His body.

"As He is, so are we in this world."

He is a New Creation—so are we.

He is the Righteousness of God—so are we.

He is an heir of God—so are we.

He is Master of the underworld—so are we in His Name.

As He has fellowship with the Father—so have we.

As He had authority in heaven and on earth—so in the Name of Jesus we have authority in heaven.

We can say to that T.B. case, "In Jesus' Name, demon, leave that body." At once the Word goes forth in heaven, and that man is delivered instantly.

Jesus had "all authority" given to Him after He arose from the dead.

He did not need that authority for Himself. That authority belongs to His body, the Church.

So we have the right to exercise this authority in doing the work that He began to do, and left us to carry on.

He said, "Greater works than these shall ye do; because I go unto the Father."

The moment He sat down at the right hand of the Father, He empowered the Church to go and do the kind of work that He was doing before His crucifixion.

He has all wisdom, and He is our wisdom.

He has authority.

We are one with Him to use that authority to glorify the Father.

Chapter XV

FRUITS OF RIGHTEOUSNESS

ROM Cor. 9:10, "And increase the fruits of your right-eousness."

This Scripture has been challenging my spirit for some time. I often wondered what the fruits of Right-eousness were.

Then I remembered the fruits of Righteousness in Jesus' life. The fruits of Righteousness were not right actions only but they were carrying out the will of His Father, speaking the words of His Father.

That meant healing the sick, feeding the multitudes, and all the other manifestations of His love toward man.

They were the fruits of Righteousness.

If we are to bear the fruits of Righteousness, they will be similar to these.

Jesus said, "I am the vine, ye are the branches."

The branch bears the same kind of fruit as the vine. It is like the vine. It is a part of the vine.

Then the fruits of Righteousness in our lives will be bless-ing and helping folks, healing their diseases, opening the Word to them, breaking the power of the Adversary over their lives, teaching them how to live in the will of the Father, teaching them how to enjoy all the fulness of His grace, and by showing forth in our daily walk a fearless fellowship with the Father, a fearless attitude toward the Adversary and all his works, a fearless mastery over circumstances.

That would be bearing fruit. That would be bearing "right-eousness fruit."

This is something utterly new to most of us.

We know about the fruits of love and the fruits of faith. We know the fruits of knowledge, but we know little of the fruits of Righteousness.

Righteousness here means the ability to stand in the Fath-er's presence without the sense of guilt or inferiority.

Fearless Faith

What mighty things could be wrought if men were con-scious of their Righteousness!

How fearless they would be in the presence of disease and sickness!

Jesus' entire public ministry was the fruit of His Righteous-ness.

He was not afraid of the Father, of Satan, of malignant diseases, or even of death. He had no fear in the presence of storms that filled other men's hearts with terror.

He was not only fearless, but He was Master.

A man said to me, "If I knew that I was what the Word says I am, I could shake the world."

But· he had never learned to believe the Word. He would believe the Word if it said that he was unworthy or if it said that he was of no value, poor, weak and faithless. He would believe that, for it had become a part of his consciousness.

He could not grasp the fact that God could recreate him and make him Righteous.

One said, "If I did not have a Sin Consciousness, I would have faith. If I had faith, I would get up from this bed perfectly healed."

Sin Consciousness had gained the mastery.

He was a Christian. He would tell you that he believed his sins had been pardoned and that he was justified.

Some would even go farther and say, "I have received the Holy Spirit and have spoken in tongues."

Yet they too are dominated by Sin Consciousness.

Why? Because the Word has never become a reality to them.

Here and there a part of the Word is real, but the great body of truth in regard to themselves is still unexplored territory.

God's Problem

The problem is this: Was God able to produce a Redemption that would redeem man from the hand of the Adversary, recreate him, make him a New Creation, and remit all that he had ever done? Could God take the sin nature out of man and in its place give him His own nature so that he could stand before Him without any Sin Consciousness, without the sense of guilt or inferiority?

Yes, He could and did provide a Redemption like that. The Pauline Revelation is the unveiling of that Redemption.

We do not find that unveiling in the four Gospels, or the book of Acts. It is only in Paul's Revelation.

In that Revelation he tells us he is going to prove to the world that Righteousness has at last become available through faith in Jesus Christ as Saviour and Redeemer.

He climaxes it by declaring, "That God might be righteous, and the righteousness of him that hath faith in Jesus."

When God becomes our Righteousness, we become so Righteous that there is "therefore now no condemnation" to us.

No one can bring a charge against us for it is God who has declared us Righteous.

The amazing fact of the New Creation is that the instant we become a New Creation, the thing that kept us in weakness and bondage, unable to stand in God's presence, has been wiped out.

In the place of our sin and our union with Satan has come union with God. Eternal Life, a new nature, and a new standing before God has come to the man who has faith in Jesus.

If that is true, we can get our prayers answered, we can use the Name of Jesus and Satan will obey us.

God has made us Righteous with His Righteousness.

2 Cor. 5:21, "Him who knew no sin he made to be sin on our behalf, that we might become the righteousness of God in him."

He has cleansed us with the blood of His own Son.

We can stand in the Father's presence now as though sin had never touched us.

It will be interesting to note some of the special fruits of Righteousness.

We will have faith in His words in our lips, just as Jesus had faith in the words of the Father in His lips.

When Jesus spoke to the sick and said, "Arise, take up thy bed and walk," the Father had given Him those words.

We have the Father's words in the Pauline Revelation and in the four Gospels.

Those words are for us to use. We can say to the sick, In the Name of Jesus Christ, come out of him," and the demon will obey because they are the Father's words spoken in our lips.

Did not Christ say, "Verily, verily, I say unto you, he that believeth on me, the works that I do shall he do also; and greater works than these shall he do; because I go unto the Father."

We can say, "By His stripes we are healed," and know that the Father will make it good.

We will have faith in the Father's words in our lips.

We will have faith in the name of Jesus in our lips.

We Are Masters

There will be a fearlessness in the presence of need and want.

We are the Righteousness of God in Christ.

The fruits of that Righteousness will be healing the sick, and breaking Satan's dominion over men. It will be the ability to unfold the Word.

The moment we become the Righteousness of God, the Spirit becomes our teacher, the Word becomes our food and our education.

We should be studying the Word, poring over it.

The Spirit will illuminate it and make it a living thing in our lips and in our hearts.

We will no longer be afraid of God, because we will realize that He is our Father.

We will go to Him with a sense of joy and rest in His presence.

It will be as natural for us to go to Him as it is for a son to go to his father.

We will find a freedom in prayer that we have never known because we will be taking our place.

We will say, "Father, we thank thee that we have a right to come into your presence, and we know that thou art pleased to have us come."

We will have faith in our own faith.

We will believe that the love which has been imparted to us by the nature of God will conquer and overcome. That love in us will be like love in Jesus. It will gain the mastery over the masses.

We will believe in the love that is in us, that it is stronger than any force that can come against us.

We will have faith in humanity, that it will respond to the appeal of love, and that we will see the fruitage from our ministry.

We will have faith in 1 Cor. 1:30, that God has made Jesus to be our wisdom and that we have in us God's wisdom.

Jesus Himself is in us as He was in Paul. We will know that He is not only our wisdom, but that He is also our Righteousness.

"But of him are ye in Christ Jesus, who was made unto us wisdom from God, and righteousness and sanctification, and redemption."

He was made unto us Righteousness.

We know of course that we are the Righteousness of God in Him.

He is now our standing with the Father. We need have no sense of guilt, no need to continually pray for forgiveness.

We should have no sense of sin because He is our Righteousness and He is in us.

His fulness, His ability is in us. It is all ours. He is our sanctification.

He is separating us from the things that would hinder us in our ministry, in our walk, in our joy in our usefulness.

He is our Redemption from the hand of the Enemy.

From this hour He is redeeming us from ignorance, failure, weakness, and from the habits that have held us in bondage.

He has become all this to us through grace.

We believe it.

We rejoice in it, and live in the fulness of it.

Chapter XVI

WORKS OF RIGHTEOUSNESS

EPH. 2:10, "For we are his workmanship, created in Christ Jesus, for good works, which God afore prepared that we should walk in them."

These good works are all planned by the Father.

There isn't a thing demanded of us that we cannot accomplish.

If He says we are "without spot or wrinkle", He is able to make us without spot or wrinkle in our conduct.

If He says that we are "holy, without blemish before Him", He has ability to present us without blemish before the Father.

The New Creation has no past.

2 Cor. 5:17, "Old things are passed away; behold, they are become new. But all these things are of God."

It is the God Life imparted to us that is producing these things.

John 6:47, "He that believeth hath eternal life."

1 John 5:13, "These things have I written unto you, that ye may know that ye have eternal life, even unto you that believe on the name of the Son of God."

We possess this Eternal Life, the nature of God, now.

If we have the nature of God, we will do the things that the nature of God would do. We are to give the nature of God right-of-way in us.

This will cause us to grow marvelously. Men will not understand it. It will be beyond their reason.

Why? Because we have let God's nature gain the ascendency in us.

I John 4:4, "Ye are of God, my little children, and have overcome them; because greater is he that is in you than he that is in the world."

These mighty Scriptures that demand a higher type of life than we have been living show that God gives us the ability to be what He demands us to be.

We who can walk into the presence of the Father at any time, who can stand in the presence of the Father without the sense of condemnation, are like a man that has vast sums of money deposited in the bank, while the country needs factories and stores opened to set the people at work. Yet he does not use his resources to help the people.

We have the resources of God at our disposal.

We have no sense of condemnation. We are perfectly free to use the Name of Jesus.

We can heal the sick. We can preach the Word with

power. We can unfold the riches of the grace of God in the Scriptures so that men and women are built up in their faith.

We have the very riches of Christ at our disposal.

We are in touch with the fulness of love and the ability of God.

There is no limit to what we can do.

We remember that Jesus said, "All things are possible with God", and "All things are possible to him that believeth'..

We link these two together and see what blessings come to the human race.

There is an Omnipotent God of love and faithfulness, and there is a vast body of people who need his ministration and blessing.

We, who are the Righteousness of God, have the key to the situation.

God cannot bless without our asking for it. We cannot ask for it with any degree of confidence unless we are assured of our Righteousness.

If one is free from the sense of guilt and condemnation, faith grows to miracle-working power.

All this is to one end, that we might bring forth fruits of Righteousness.

"The works that I do shall ye do also", said Jesus. He blessed the world—so will we. He fed the multitudes—so will we. He healed the sick—so will we. He comforted the broken-hearted—so will we.

He gave encouragement. He gave strength. He gave Himself. We will bear the same kind of fruit.

Heb. 10:1-4 "For the law having a shadow of the good things to come, not the very image of the things, can never with the same sacrifices year by year, which they offer continually, make perfect them that draw nigh. Else would they not have ceased to be offered? because the worshippers, having been once cleansed, would have had no more consciousness of sins. But in those sacrifices there is a remembrance made of sins year by year. For it is impossible that the blood of bulls and goats should take away sins."

They had a continual consciousness of sins. Jesus was the end of sacrifice.

We, who have been recreated, have no more consciousness of sins.

Why? Because we are the Righteousness of God in Him.

Heb. 10:12-13, "But he, when he had offered one sacrifice for sins forever, sat down on the right hand of God; henceforth expecting till his enemies be made the footstool of his feet."

He sat down at the right hand of God.

The high priest who carried the blood of bulls and goats into the Holy of Holies could not sit down because he knew that next year he would have to return again.

Jesus made but one sacrifice.

Heb. 10:14, "For by one offering he hath perfected for ever them that are sanctified."

Our Righteousness, our recreation, our sonship, are all perfect.

Heb. 10:38, "But my righteous one shall live by faith."

How is he going to walk? By faith.

He has become the Righteousness of God in Christ. From now on his walk is a faith walk.

It means walking in the Word. He lives the Word, as Joshua lived the Word when he led the priests into the Jordan.

He walked according to the word of the Angel of the Covenant.

We are walking as Jesus walked. He is the Surety of the New Covenant.

We are walking according to the Word.

When God said to Moses, "Lift up thy rod over the sea", Moses did so and the waters receded. Moses walked in the word of the Angel.

We are to walk in the Word of this New Covenant.

As we walk in this New Covenant Word, we will walk in love, we will walk in fellowship with the Father, we will walk in God's ability.

We will take Jesus' place and we will do Righteousness. We will destroy the works of the Adversary, just as Jesus destroyed the works of the Adversary.

We go on unveiling the riches of Christ to others until their hearts break and they say, "We want Him too."

The moment they accept Christ, the work of the Adversary is broken over their lives.

Righteousness is going forth as a light. The ability of God is being unveiled to the weak. Jesus is becoming a living thing in the lives of men and women.

Miracles are an every day occurence in their lives.

They are unveiling to the world that Christianity is supernatural.

Chapter XVII

CROWN OF RIGHTEOUSNESS

AUL tells us in 2 Tim. 4:8 of the "crown of righteousness."

Righteousness means the ability to stand in the Father's presence without the sense of inferiority or Sin Consciousness.

It is to be the crown of the believer's life.

I have been greatly exercised of late about this fact of our acting the part of a Righteous man.

In I John 2:29, the Spirit through John tells us about doing Righteousness. That means doing the works of a man who has no sense of guilt or fear of God, fear of disease, fear of circumstance, or fear of man.

Doing the work of a Righteous man would mean a fearless life of intercession, a fearless testimony of the grace of God, a fearless walk in the presence of the world, and a fearless fellowship with the Father.

It is using our Righteousness as Jesus used it.

I know this is a new thought, but it is a suggestive one.

The very theme of the book of Romans is the showing of God's ability to set a man right with Him, to declare him Righteous and to make him Righteous so that he can stand in the Father's presence without the sense of guilt.

He triumphantly shouts, "There is therefore now no condemnation to them that are in Christ Jesus." Rom. 8:1.

He asks this question, "Who shall lay anything to the charge of God's elect? It is God that justifieth: who is he that condemneth?"

God did not fail in His Redemptive work. Jesus did not fail. The Spirit has not failed in His work. The Word has not failed to make good in every case where it has been used.

Let us begin at the basis of it.

Isaiah 32:17 is a prophetic statement in regard to Righteousness.

"And the work of righteousness shall be peace."

It is the peace of God which passes all understanding. It fills the heart the moment we become New Creations.

The moment we receive Eternal Life, that moment we become the Righteousness of God.

We are made out of Righteousness and holiness of truth. Eph. 4.24.

"And the effect of righteousness, quietness and confidence forever."

Just the moment we are justified or made Righteous in

Christ, that moment quietness comes and confidence fills our hearts. The rest of God, the peace of God, the quietness of God fills our spirits.

Is. 62:1 throws added light on God's purposes in Redemption.

"For Zion's sake will I not hold my peace, and for Jerusalem's sake I will not rest, until her righteousness go forth as brightness, and her salvation as a lamp that burneth."

He is not going to hold His peace until the hour comes when man can be the Righteousness of God in Christ.

That Righteousness is going forth as brightness, and her salvation, the New Creation, as a lamp that burneth.

How true that was on the day of Pentecost!

Rom. 3:26 (Marginal Translation), "That he might himself be righteous, and the righteousness of him that hath faith in Jesus."

We have been justified freely by His grace through the Redemption that is in Christ Jesus.

2 Cor. 5:21 has become a reality.

"Him who knew no sin he made to be sin on our behalf; that we might become the righteousness of God in Him."

Jesus was made sin with our sins. He was made weak with our weaknesses. He was made a failure with our failures. He was made sick with our sicknesses. He was made unrighteous with our unrighteousness.

After He put all that away, satisfied every claim of Justice, was made alive—made Righteous in Spirit, then by the New Birth He made us the Righteousness of God in Him.

We stand before God as His own Righteousness.

We are created in Christ Jesus.

It is all of God—"not of works lest any man should boast. For we are his workmanship, created in Christ Jesus." Eph. 2:8-10.

How it thrills the heart to think that it is not of man. Man has no glory in it. It is all of God. It is the grace of God unveiled. It is the love of God mightily exercised to set us right with Himself.

Now we can understand 1 Cor. 1:30, "But of him are ye in Christ Jesus, who was made unto us wisdom from God, and righteousness and sanctification, and redemption."

All this is from God.

All this belongs to us.

"He that glorieth, let him glory in the Lord."

God is satisfied with what He did in the New Creation as He was satisfied with what He did in the first Creation.

He is not ashamed to be called our Father.

Jesus is not ashamed to be called our Lord and Saviour, our Redeemer and our Righteousness.

They are not ashamed of what they have done.

Rom. 8:1, "There is therefore now no condemnation to them that are in Christ Jesus."

33rd verse, "Who shall lay anything to the charge of God's elect?"

Who elected them? God did.

There is only one person in the universe that can bring a charge against us, and that is Jesus.

Jesus will not bring a charge against us because it was He who died for us. Now He ever lives to make intercession for us at the Father's right hand.

Who recreated us? God did.

Who gave us Eternal Life? God did.

Who made us sons and daughters of God? God did.

It is all of God.

We are accepted in the Beloved, and the Father rejoices over it.

We are His own children.

Chapter XVIII

SOME RIGHTEOUSNESS REALITIES

E do not grow in Righteousness. We are made Righteous, and Righteousness is credited to us. God Himself is our Righteousness and He made Jesus to be Righteousness unto us.

There is no such thing as growth in Righteousness.

There is growth in the knowledge of what Righteousness means. There is growth in acting as though we were Righteous. There is growth in faith in our Righteousness.

Very few people have any faith in their Righteousness in Christ.

They have faith in their weakness and their lack of ability, but few have any faith in the thing that God has made them to be.

This is an unhappy fact. Until we have confidence in our own standing before the Father, in our own Righteousness in Christ, we will never have faith that will bring blessing to ourselves and others.

Faith is destroyed by Sin Consciousness.

Faith is built up and made invincible by Righteousness Consciousness.

This entire problem rests upon our estimation of the Word. If we have a low estimation of the Word, then we will have a low estimation of our Righteousness in Christ.

If we have a low estimation of the Word, our faith will be weak and vacillating. But if we believe the Word, rest on the Word, know that no Word from God is untrue and that God cannot lie, then our faith becomes strong.

When we say that God cannot lie we mean that the Word cannot lie. It is the Word with which we are dealing.

The Word is the contract, the Covenant, the legal instrument with which we have to do. It is more than a legal document. It is a living document.

It becomes a living force in our lives as we act upon it.

A low estimate of the New Covenant or the New Testament will bring a low estimate of the work that Christ did. A low estimate of the Word and of the work that Christ did is bound to react in our lives.

Men and women will see at once that there is something weak and inefficient in our lives.

When we believe Rom. 4:25, it will be manifested in our lives, in our conduct.

"Who was delivered up on the account of our trespasses and was raised because we were declared righteous."

People will feel it in our conversation.

But if we doubt the efficacy of His finished work, every phase of our life will show it.

The reason people cannot get their healing is because of a low estimation of the Word and of the finished work of Christ.

When we have the proper estimation of the finished work of Jesus Christ, we know that "By His stripes we are healed," and we need no one to pray for us.

We know we are healed, and with joy we thank Him for it.

All this trying to be worthy, trying to be Righteous, crying and agonizing before the Lord, is the product of a low estimation of the integrity of the Word of God.

When we know that the Word is true, that we are what the Word says we are, and that we can do all the Word says we can, we begin at once to take our place, assert our authority, and enjoy our privileges in Christ.

We grow in grace.

Grace is love unvelied, love in action. It is love doing things.

We can grow in that. We can let love dominate us. Then we will reveal Jesus in our conduct.

We can grow in love until our whole life is saturated with it, until every motive will be born of it, until every word will have its fragrance.

We are Righteous from the time we are Born Again.

Faith grows as we walk in the Word.

We grow in knowledge of our Righteousness, what it can mean to us, and its vast privileges and responsibilities.

We do not grow in sonship, though we may grow in the knowledge of what sonship means.

Perhaps the clearest definition of what we are in Christ is given in Heb. 10:38, "But my righteous one shall live by faith, and if he shrink back, my soul hath no pleasure in him."

God calls the church His "righteous one."

He speaks of us individually as His righteous one.

If we draw back into the Sense Realm of dead works, we rob Him of the joy that belongs to Him.

Man's Real Need Is Met

Jesus in His great High Priestly prayer in John 17:3 said, "And this is life eternal ,that they should know thee the only true God, and him whom thou didst send, even Jesus Christ."

The word "true" means "real".

"That they should know thee the only real God."

We may have many theories and facts which men have gathered concerning God, but we will never know Him as a Father until we receive Eternal Life.

We will never know the real Christ until we receive Eternal Life. We may know about Him, may have read volumes about Him, but until we receive Eternal Life we will never know Him in reality.

Jesus is the light of the world. He is the Life. The Life is the oil which, when ignited by love, gives light.

This love God and this love Christ are both living realities. He said, "I am the way, and the reality, and the life."

Real philosophy is a search after God. The moment the philosopher finds Eternal Life, he stops being a philosopher and becomes a realist.

God is love. Eternal Life is the love nature of God.

When we receive Eternal Life, we receive His love nature. Then that love nature begins to dominate us, and gain the ascendency in our lives.

1 John 4:16 tells us about abiding in love, making our home in love.

"And we know and have believed the love which God hath in our case. God is love; and he that abideth in love abideth in God, and God abideth in him."

It is a love life. We are beginning to walk in Him and with Him. It makes a companion of Him.

"If a man love me, he will keep my word: and my Father will love him, and we will come unto him and make our abode with him." John 14:23.

Can we ask for anything more beautiful than that?

Jesus and the Father will come and make their home with us—no matter how humble it is.

They will make it beautiful. They will make it a safe place for children to be born. No quarreling, no bitterness, no divorces can ever come into the home where Jesus lives.

This home life with Jesus is the mother of faith. It makes our home relationship beautiful.

We meet dishonesty and faithlessness without saying an unkind word. We enter into a new kind of life where we never think of being neglected, forgotten or ignored. We never remember anything that is unkind.

This new love is life: this new life is love.

We forgive those who are dishonest because this new life has taken possession of us.

We are taking Jesus' place in the earth. We are loving as Jesus would love. We are giving as Jesus would give. We are as helpful as the Master would be in our place.

We live with Him. His love is our love. His strength is our strength. His ability is ours.

We are His own love slaves.

We love Him because He loves us.

Chapter XIX

OUR NEW FREEDOM

HERE has been coming to the hearts of our people a new sense of freedom in Christ. It is a new sense of freedom in the Father's presence.

It is the abandonment to love.

There has come a new freedom in love, a new freedom in the Word.

For years we were like a boat land-locked in a narrow lagoon. Now we are sailing on the bosom of the mighty ocean.

There is a new sense of superiority over the circumstances that terrified and held us in bondage, the consciousness of that tremendous reality—"Greater is he that is in you than he that is in the world."

It has given us a new consciousness of superiority over disease and pain.

Sickness held us in bondage of fear and dread, but we are no longer afraid of it.

It has been conquered.

The Name of Jesus is greater.

Our relationship with the Father makes us greater.

We are sons and daughters of God Almighty.

We are partakers of His nature.

We are members of His household.

We are as near to His heart as Jesus was when He walked the earth.

There has come to us a new sense of oneness with Christ.

That joint heirship is a reality. It is more than the clasp of a hand. It is more than an embrace.

It is a union. It is an organic oneness.

A spiritual harmony flows from it. It is a masterful thing. We are one with Him!

The branch discovers its union with the Vine. It abandons worry and care.

The branch says, "I no longer worry whether the bud will blossom, whether the blossom will turn into fruit. I have no anxious care. The vine takes care of it all. The vine dresser and I are so utterly one now that I rest quietly in the embrace of the vine."

The new sense of authority in Christ, born out of slavery into victory, out of weakness into the ability to use the Name with authority, has come to us.

A new strange sense of fellowship has come.

A joy that only came intermittently now lives with us permanently.

But one of the sweetest things is the new freshness of the Word, its literalness, its absoluteness, that we had not known before.

As I dictate, it seems to me as though the Master were here and if I should open my eyes I would see Him standing before us.

I long to throw my arms about His feet and kiss the scars where the nails once held Him to the Cross.

My Lord! My wonderful Risen Lord!

God and Jesus are speaking out of the Word in a new sense of reality.

There is a "nowness" about the Word.

It is so beautifully personal.

He is speaking to me. It is my Lord asking me to come into conference with Him.

He, who was once made sin for me, has made me His Righteousness now, and by that wondrous act He has lifted me from the mud and slime of failure to sit with Him upon the throne.

I cannot grasp it . My heart looks in wonder and amazement at my surroundings.

An angel whispers, "He is a son of God. He is a joint heir with our Master."

We are what He says we are. Being what we are, we can act for Him. We can take His place here on the earth among men.

The new sense of mastery that comes from our relationship with Him lets us into the throne room.

We have passed the portals of fear. We stand fearless in the presence of our Master and our Lord.

From now on we are under orders from heaven. Jesus is our Lord.

Joyfully we sing, "He is our shepherd, we shall not want."

God is now our Father. He is for us.

Not only is He for us, but He is also with us.

Not only is He with us, but He is in us.

We are in absolute union with Christ.

Satan's dominion over us is broken.

We stand free in the fulness of His life.

Chapter XX

SOME WAYS THAT RIGHTEOUSNESS IS USED

 N. 2 Cor. 6:7-8, we read "In the word of truth, in the power of God; by the armor of righteousness on the right hand and on the left, by glory and dishonor, by evil report and good report;"

Righteousness is an armor in the presence of the most terrific onslaught.

Satan's arrows cannot pierce through the armor of Righteousness.

We are the wearers of Righteousness.

Eph. 6:14, "Stand therefore, having girded your loins with truth, and having put on the breast plate of righteousness."

How do we put on Righteousness? By confession.

We confess that He is our Righteousness.

We live our confession.

We fearlessly face the forces of darkness with the consciousness that no arrow can pierce the breast-plate of Righteousness.

2 Tim. 4:8, "Henceforth there is laid up for me the crown of righteousness, which the Lord, the righteous judge, shall give to me at that day; and not to me only, but also to all them that have loved his appearing."

This crown goes to the believer who has wrought in Righteousness for the Master.

If we walk in this new Righteousness sense, and do as John tells us in I John 2:29, we become "doers of Righteousness."

"If ye know that he is righteous, ye know that every one also that doeth righteousness is begotten of him."

We can do the works of Righteousness.

What does it mean? A fearless prayer life. A fearless giving. A fearless testimony. A fearless acting on the Word,—laying hands on the sick, casting out demons.

We know that as He is, so are we in this world.

We know that His Righteousness has made us Righteous.

It gives us access to His very throne.

We fearlessly take our place.

We are doing the things that a Righteous man would do in our place.

We are witnessing as a Righteous man would witness.

We get our reward and crown for our fearless confession before the world.

I want to be sure that you are getting your share of the blessings that come to those who "do Righteousness."

Rom. 5:17-21 ushers us into the real Holy of Holies of Righteousness.

May I give you Weymouth's translation.

"For if, through the transgression of the one individual, Death made use of the one individual to seize the sovereignty, all the more shall those who receive God's overflowing grace and gift of righteousness reign as kings in Life through the one individual, Jesus Christ."

We reign as kings in the realm of Eternal Life.

We take the initiative out of the hands of the enemy on the ground of this gift of Righteousness which God has given us.

Then in the 21st verse, "But where sin increased, grace has overflowed; in order that as sin has exercised kingly sway in inflicting death, so grace, too, may, exercise kingly sway in bestowing a righteousness which results in the Life of the Ages through Jesus Christ our Lord."

I think that is one of the most masterly translations ever given.

We reign as kings in this realm of life where we have served as slaves in the realm of spiritual death.

We have been held in bondage as a race ever since the Fall of man.

Now we have discovered this gold mine of Righteousness that makes us reign as kings, that gives us authority over the works of the Adversary, that uncovers the very wealth and riches of the Father's grace.

We now exercise kingly sway in this realm of Righteousness over the forces that would hold us in bondage.

The Effect of Righteousness

"Then shall the righteous shine forth as the sun in the kingdom of their Father." Matt. 13:43.

What a confession from the lips of the Father that those who have been made Righteous with His own Righteousness in the New Covenant shall shine forth as the sun!

Now they walk in the fulness of the dignity and reality of the Father's own Righteousness. They have been made Righteous by the Father himself.

Righteousness In the Father's Estimation

Rom. 3:26, "That he might himself be righteous, and the righteousness of him that hath faith in Jesus."

God is the Righteousness of the man who has faith in Jesus Christ as his Saviour and Lord.

The Creator of the universe becomes our Righteousness. He gives us the ability to stand in His presence as though sin had never been. He becomes our Sponsor.

2 Cor. 5:21, speaking of Jesus, "Him who knew no sin God

made to become sin on our behalf; that we might become the righteousness of God in him."

By the New Birth, we have become the very Righteousness of God in Christ. He is the Author and Creator of this Righteousness.

He made us to be His own Righteousness.

To give us confidence and assurance in our daily walk, He out of His great love has become our Righteousness.

Eph. 2:8-10, "For by grace have ye been saved (or healed) through faith; and that not of yourselves, it is the gift of God; not of works, that no man should glory. For we are his workmanship, created in Christ Jesus."

What He creates and what He makes is beautiful in His sight.

We are His love poem.

We, who have become New Creations, have the ability to stand before the throne of grace with joy, with pride in the Righteousness that He has given us.

Not only can we stand before the Throne, but we can also face Satan unafraid.

We are masters.

We can face the raging sea as Jesus did, and know that it is our servant.

We can face the hungry multitudes as Jesus faced it, and know that five loaves and two little fishes when touched by love will multiply until the crowds are satisfied.

We can stand before a lost world knowing that Jesus' sacrifice on Calvary and His victory over death, hell and the grave are all that lost world needs.

No one has a better Righteousness than we have.
No one has a better Saviour than we have.
No one has a better Eternal Life than we have.
No one has a better standing with the Father than we have,
No one has a better right to the use of the Name of Jesus than we have.

No one can get closer to the heart of the Father than we can.

We are what He says we are.
We are in the Beloved.
We are the Father's own heart dream.
Let us not be like those Peter speaks of in 2 Peter 1:9-10.

"For he that lacketh these things is blind, seeing only what is near, having forgotten the cleansing from his old sins. Wherefore, brethren, give the more diligence to make your calling and election sure: for if ye do these things, ye shall never stumble."

When he speaks of making our election sure, it does not mean that it is making it sure in heaven. It is sure there. But it is to make you more sure-footed in the Way, to give you the quiet confidence that belongs to the children of God.

1 Cor. 2:12 may help us a little.

"But we received, not the spirit of the world, but the spirit which is from God; that we might know the things that were freely given to us of God."

The object of this message is that those who read it may enjoy their inheritance in Christ, that they may enjoy all that belongs to them and not be slow to take advantage of their rights.

WHAT DO YOU SAY?

What are the reactions in your spirit?

Has it been a profitable journey that we have had together?

Have you found the liberty and joy that we promised when you started?

If you have, then you have found a Responsibility.

You are a debtor to others; you have the Light, it will be necessary for you to tell them about it.

Why not have a group meet once a week in your home and use our books as textbooks.

Start a lending library in your home.

Send for our books. Read them. Let the mighty truths gain the ascendency, and then you will become a blessing as you have always desired to be in Christ.

Inspiring Books
by E. W. KENYON

THE BIBLE IN THE LIGHT
OF OUR REDEMPTION
  A Basic Bible Course

ADVANCED BIBLE COURSE
  Studies in the Deeper Life

THE HIDDEN MAN OF THE HEART

WHAT HAPPENED
  From the Cross to the Throne

NEW CREATIONS REALITIES

IN HIS PRESENCE
  The Secret of Prayer

THE TWO KINDS OF LIFE

THE FATHER AND HIS FAMILY
  The Story of Man's Redemption

THE WONDERFUL NAME OF JESUS
  Our Rights and Privileges in Prayer

JESUS THE HEALER
  Has Brought Healing to Thousands

KENYON'S LIVING POEMS

THE NEW KIND OF LOVE

THE TWO KINDS OF FAITH

THE TWO KINDS OF RIGHTEOUSNESS

THE BLOOD COVENANT

THE TWO KINDS OF KNOWLEDGE

SIGN POSTS ON THE ROAD TO SUCCESS

IDENTIFICATION

Order From:
KENYON'S GOSPEL PUBLISHING SOCIETY
P.O. Box 973, Lynnwood, Washington 98046